D0507964

MEALS TO ENJOY FROM YOUR FREEZER

by Audrey Ellis

HAMLYN
LONDON · NEW YORK · SYDNEY · TORONTO

Contents

The author gratefully acknowledges the help of:
RESEARCH EDITORS: GWYNEDD HINDMARSH & ANN SCUTCHER
Special series of food preparation photographs taken by:
Butter Information Council
Ann Smith and Frigidaire Division of General Motors Limited
Blue Band Bureau
Birds Eye Foods Limited
Fruit Producers Council

Introduction

In response to numerous requests, the publishers have decided to reproduce *Home Guide to Deep Freezing* as two paper-back volumes.

The first volume, under the title *All About Home Freezing*, deals with choosing, buying and filling a freezer. This second volume, which has been considerably expanded, contains advice on menu-planning and many recipes for appetising meals from the freezer.

There are three advantages which, when you invest in a freezer, you will soon discover.

Firstly, you will be able to buy commercially frozen food and fresh meat in bulk at considerably reduced prices and save a substantial sum month by month towards the initial cost of the freezer. Deliveries made straight to your door by refrigerated van will make frequent shopping expeditions a thing of the past, saving your money, time and energy.

Secondly, freezing your own garden produce, or fresh fruit and vegetables you can buy cheaply at certain times of the year, will represent another economy. You will find that you always have plenty of food in stock and your first reaction when planning meals for the day soon tends to be – "What is in my freezer?" rather than – "What must I buy today?" But there is a further bonus in time and money saved by the use of the freezer for preserving home-cooked dishes.

The average housewife spends more time each day cooking than in any other task. Breakfast, packed meals, elevenses, lunch, tea, dinner, suppers and snacks – there seems no end to the number of meals to be prepared each day and no escape from the kitchen for the harassed housewife. Cooking always seems to coincide with other important domestic chores, just when you are busiest – getting the children off to school, helping them with their homework, or putting the little ones to bed! Or if you are a working wife, it seems to swallow up all your spare time.

This is where the freezer can help you to plan and cook ahead. A great deal of time can be saved in repetitive preparation tasks by cooking in much larger quantities and freezing a number of meals for future use, as well as having one ready to eat at once. You can do most of your cooking at the time of day when you are free to give your whole attention to it. Many housewives seem to find that this is during the early afternoon, by the way, but working wives often prefer to have a big cooking spree over the weekend.

In fact, by partly stocking your freezer with cooked dishes which will include pre-cooked sauces and prepared items such as uncooked pastry and biscuit dough, you can alter the entire pattern of catering for the family to reduce the hard work involved to an absolute minimum.

You will find chain cooking, which is fully described in Chapter Two, is another fascinating adventure in cooking for a freezer owner.

It is such a boon to have stocks of your own home-made sauces always available, to dress up a pasta dish or transform left-overs into a creamy ragoût. Just see how many ready-to-cook and fully prepared dishes you can chain-cook with chicken, for example. One cake-making session each month will keep the family well supplied with delicious fresh cakes, even elaborate iced ones. And one sandwich-making session will cover all demands for packed meals, even rations for the children's friends who drop in to play and stay over tea-time.

It is a good idea to make up packs of assorted sandwiches for freezing. If someone has a special preference or dislike, write his name on packs which contain no peanut butter, or plenty of sardine spread, according to individual taste. Sandwiches take about $2\frac{1}{2}$ hours to thaw, which means that they're usually just ready for eating by the time they're needed. If needed more quickly, spread them on a plate to thaw.

You will soon become accustomed to the convenience of serving commercially frozen foods more often because buying them in bulk is more economical. You may then feel like experimenting to find new, adventurous ways of serving them.

It is now so much easier to find suppliers of bulk frozen foods who will give you a very prompt, reasonable and satisfactory service, no matter where you live, that I have felt it necessary to include a special new chapter on making more of these convenience foods.

Various different services are rapidly becoming available to housewives who want to buy some or most household items in bulk, and take advantage of the big savings this kind of buying makes possible. You may like to buy only frozen products such as fruit, vegetables, pastry and prepared dishes, and there is now the excellent Birds Eye Home Freezer Service throughout the country to suit your needs. Other firms supply ready frozen products, plus butcher's meat, and even wine in bulk, and also offer freezers at a worthwhile discount. Kitchen Range Ltd., give this very full type of service, for example, in the South-Eastern region.

The freezer is a true friend to every housewife who tries (however spasmodically) to follow a slimming diet. It is all to easy to fill up on bread, rolls or biscuits when no more suitable food is available, but it is just the food dieters need which occupies most space in the freezer. Fruit, vegetables, meat, poultry – you can even freeze individual portions of cooked lean meat and chicken specially labelled for yourself, prepared without any starchy ingredients. This method comes in handy when any member of the family is temporarily (or perhaps as in the case of a diabetic, or a person with a constant weight problem) on a special diet. You can keep a supply of food on hand specially labelled and parcelled, to enable you to serve this one person an entirely different meal, with the minimum of trouble.

You may also find it handy to make use of a special one-portion pack for someone who has to eat at different times from the rest of the household. Sometimes unusual working hours, or a hobby that keeps someone away from family meal-times, causes this problem. When you have a big cooking spree, you could very easily fill a batch of foil dinner plates with individual portions of a meat or poultry dish.

Entertaining one's friends ought to be a pleasure but many housewives secretly feel that the enjoyment is very much diminished by the additional hard work and anxiety involved in catering. It embarrasses any hostess to let her guests see that preparing a meal for them is really a chore. It may well deprive them of her company for a good deal of their visit. With a choice of ready-cooked food always to hand in your freezer it is much more of a pleasure to cater for guests, even unexpected ones.

Big parties, where there is a lot of food to prepare, often leave the hostess too exhausted and harassed to enjoy herself. Where there is storage space available in the freezer, many dishes can be made during leisure hours, days or even more than a week beforehand. This applies to fancy sandwiches, canapés, hors d'oeuvre and soups as well as main dishes and sweets. If you prepare more than is needed you can cut down on wastage by keeping extra supplies in the refrigerator and returning them to the freezer if they are not needed. If dinner-party guests cancel on the day, you have a wonderful meal in store which need not be used for months to come; or, it can be served to guests you did not expect, tomorrow.

To sum up, careful use of the freezer should enable you to save time and money and enjoy a far greater range of menus than ever before. It is particularly rewarding when you have made a good "buy" and at the same time provided trouble-free meals for weeks or even months ahead. But the amount of time and effort you save is undoubtedly governed by forethought and planning on your part.

Audrey Ellis

Chapter One
Cooking ahead—
the 'eat one,
freeze two' plan

This section is devoted entirely to providing food for the day-to-day needs of the family. All of the king-size recipes found here are intended to give three complete meals, each one large enough to serve a family of four people. They can easily be adapted to meet your own particular needs – increasing the amounts by half as much again, for example, if your's is a family of six.

Cooking in bulk

The most workable plan seems to be to cook your main meal requirements once a week by preparing two main dishes, each in sufficient quantity to serve four people, three times. This will make a total of six complete meals for four people. One meal, say a liver casserole, is served straight away: a second meal, perhaps using lamb chops, will be refrigerated until it can be eaten the next day; which leaves four meals, two of each kind to be frozen. You will already have a good assortment of meals in the freezer so that you can choose from these for the rest of the week, ensuring that you don't have to eat liver casserole and lamb chops the whole week through!

It is a good notion to give each complete meal a slight variation before freezing – or eating – it. If you make a steak and kidney casserole, you can give that day's meal a pastry crust, and the two meals destined for the freezer can be given trimmings to make them a little different (for example, cobbler topping).

You will already have noticed that six meals are prepared each week, while there are seven days to be dealt with! This isn't an oversight, but it has been assumed that on at least one day out of every week, you will be invited to someone else's home for a meal, or perhaps friends will be coming to you, in which case you will not be feeding them from the family-meal section of the freezer. Your husband might unexpectedly take you out to a restaurant meal or bring home something for dinner!

The dishes you decide to prepare and freeze each week can depend on the foodstuffs that happen to be a particularly good buy at the time. For example, chicken or lamb dishes when they are especially cheap. Many people are often deterred from buying big, deliciously juicy cuts of ham and gammon because they feel that they are going to be eating ham for days on end. Now you can buy and cook it, eat some of the ham straight away and freeze the remainder, made into all kinds of interesting dishes.

Soup is another wonderful family stand-by and nothing you buy, however good, is quite the equivalent of home-made soup. Serve it with hot toast and home-made pâté for a family lunch or supper.

Desserts can be whipped out of the freezer in no time – frozen purées are excellent for emergency desserts, so too is frozen fruit, which can be served with little cupcakes also stored in the freezer.

Individual dinners find their place in this section, for sometimes a member of the family is going to eat a solitary meal – either because he is going to be late or because everyone else has gone out! Use small quantities left over from bulk cooking for single portions, packed in foil plates. Incidentally it may be a little expensive to invest in aluminium foil plates for individual plate dinners, but if they are carefully treated they can be re-used and so minimise the cost.

Before preparing food for the freezer, the following points are worth noting.

Seasonings such as salt and pepper tend to increase their flavour when frozen, so use sparingly.

The same rule applies to celery.

The flavour of onion diminishes – add more than you would normally.

Sweet herbs tend to take on a musty flavour after being stored for some time, so add them to the dish when reheating.

When thawing food with potato topping, uncover the dish to prevent the potato from becoming glutinous.

In dishes which are not reheated after thawing, cream may be added before freezing. In dishes which are to be reheated cream should be omitted and added prior to serving.

Because sauces have a tendency to separate when frozen, always beat well when you are reheating them.

Any cooked chicken dish can equally well be made with cooked turkey.

Buckling Pâté
3 large bucklings
6 oz. butter, softened
1 clove of garlic, crushed
juice of 2 lemons
freshly ground pepper

Put bucklings in boiling water for 1 minute, so that skin can be removed easily. Remove skin and bones. Pound flesh with a wooden spoon and blend together with butter. Add crushed garlic and lemon juice. Season to taste.
To freeze:
Put the pâté into 3 foil dishes, smooth the tops and seal with double thickness of foil.
To prepare for serving:
Thaw at room temperature, for 3–4 hours. Turn out of the container and cut into quarters. Serve with toast.

Makes 3 servings for 4.

Country Pâté
12 oz. pigs' liver
8 oz. fat bacon
1 onion, peeled and chopped
1 clove garlic, chopped
2 oz. butter
salt and pepper to taste
½ pint well-seasoned white sauce

Fry liver, bacon, onion and garlic in butter for about 10 minutes, gently. Remove from heat and mince or put in a blender. Season with salt and pepper. Combine the liver mixture with the sauce. Turn into a 1½-pint greased terrine or pie dish, cover with a lid or foil and place in a baking tin of hot water. Bake in moderate oven (350 deg. F. – Gas Mark 4), for 1 hour. Cover with foil, stand kitchen weights on top and leave overnight in the refrigerator.
To freeze:
Turn out of the dish, cut into slices and stack with pieces of foil between slices. Wrap in double or heavy duty foil. Seal and freeze.
To prepare for serving:
Unwrap the required number of slices. Allow approximately 1 hour for thawing. Serve with hot toast.

Makes 3 servings for 4.

Chicken Liver Pâté
3 oz. butter
12 oz. chicken livers
salt and pepper, to taste
¼ teaspoon powdered mace

Melt 1 oz. of the butter in a frying pan, add the chicken livers and cook gently for 5 minutes. Pass the livers through a fine mincer, melt the remaining butter and add to the chicken livers with the rest of the ingredients.
To freeze:
Press into 3 foil pie dishes, seal with double or heavy duty foil *or* store individual portions using the following method: Chill the pâté in the refrigerator, turn out of the foil pie dishes and cut into quarters. Stack the slices with dividing pieces of foil or moisture-vapour-proof paper between each. Wrap in moisture-vapour-proof paper and seal.

To prepare for serving:
Thaw, covered, at room temperature for approximately 1 hour.

Makes 3 servings for 4.

Bacon Pâté
3 oz. butter
1 large onion, finely chopped
1½ lb. cooked bacon, minced
1 tablespoon chopped parsley, blanched
1 level tablespoon freshly made mustard
½ teaspoon Worcestershire sauce

Melt the butter in a saucepan and gently fry the onion in it. Combine with the remaining ingredients. Spread the mixture evenly in a 2 lb. loaf tin, smooth the top and chill in the refrigerator for 2 hours.

To freeze:
Turn the pâté out of the loaf tin. Cut into 12 slices and stack with foil or moisture-vapour-proof paper dividers between the slices. Wrap in double or heavy duty foil or moisture-vapour-proof paper, seal and freeze.

To prepare for serving:
Take the required number of slices out of the package. Thaw at room temperature allowing approximately 1 hour.

Makes 3 servings for 4.

Taramasalata
12 oz. smoked cod's roe
¼ pint olive oil
juice of 1 lemon
black pepper, freshly ground
1 teaspoon very finely chopped onion
2 tablespoons chopped parsley, blanched

Remove the skin from the roe and discard. Put the roe in a bowl with 5 tablespoons of the oil. Allow to stand for 10 minutes. Pass the mixture through a fine sieve or liquidise in a blender. Add the lemon juice. Beat in the remaining olive oil, a tablespoonful at a time. Add the remaining ingredients.

To freeze:
Pack into individual foil pie dishes. Smooth the tops and seal with double or heavy duty foil. Freeze.

To prepare for serving:
Thaw at room temperature allowing approximately 1 hour. Serve on toast as an appetiser or savoury.

Makes 3 servings for 4.

Winter Vegetable Soup
4 sticks celery, thinly sliced
8 oz. parsnips, cut into ¼-inch dice
8 oz. turnips, cut into ¼-inch dice
2 onions, peeled and finely sliced
bouquet garni *plus* 6 peppercorns
4 pints chicken stock *or*
    4 stock cubes plus water
4 oz. mushrooms, finely sliced

Put all vegetables, except the mushrooms, into a saucepan. Tie bouquet garni and peppercorns in muslin and place in pan. Add the stock and simmer for 20 minutes. Add mushrooms and continue to simmer for another 10 minutes.

To freeze:
Cool and remove the herbs. Pack into 1½-pint containers, leaving ½–1-inch headspace.

To prepare for serving:
Immerse container in hot water to remove contents. Reheat gently in a covered saucepan. Dilute, if liked. Correct the seasoning.

Makes 3 servings for 4.

Barbecue Sauce
2 oz. butter
2 large onions, peeled and chopped
8 tablespoons Worcestershire sauce
8 tablespoons cider or wine vinegar
2 tablespoons brown table sauce
2 oz. sugar
2 pints water

Melt butter in a saucepan and sauté onion. Add other ingredients and simmer, covered, for 20 minutes. Uncover, then boil rapidly to reduce by one third.

To freeze:
Cool. Strain into 3 ½-pint containers.

To prepare for serving:
Immerse the container in hot water. Turn out into a saucepan, simmer gently. Makes 1½-pints.

Barbecued Meat Sauce

4 medium onions, peeled and chopped
3 cloves garlic, crushed
1 head celery, trimmed and chopped
2 oz. lard *or* dripping
4 lb. minced beef
4 teaspoons salt
½ teaspoon pepper
3 tablespoons Worcestershire sauce
¾ pint tomato ketchup

Fry the onion, garlic and celery gently in the fat in a large pan. Gradually add the minced beef and stir until all the meat has browned. Add the salt, pepper, Worcestershire sauce and ketchup. Simmer gently for 20 minutes. Skim off any excess fat.

To freeze:
Cool quickly. Spoon the mixture into 3 1½-pint containers. Seal, label and freeze.

To prepare for serving:
Immerse the container in hot water, to allow the mixture to slip out of the container into a pan for heating. This sauce can be served with all types of pasta or with rice to make a main meal. It can be heated while the rice or pasta is cooking. Makes 4½-pints.

Tomato Sauce

4 oz. onion, chopped
2 cloves garlic, *crushed with* 1 teaspoon salt
1 tablespoon oil
3 tablespoons tomato purée
2 2-lb. 3-oz. cans tomatoes
2 tablespoons castor sugar
3–4 parsley stalks
1 bay leaf
salt and pepper to taste

Sauté the onion and garlic in oil until soft. Stir in the tomato purée, canned tomatoes (with the juice) and sugar. Tie the parsley stalks and bay leaf with thread and add to the ingredients in the pan; add the salt and pepper. Bring to the boil, reduce the heat then cover with a lid and simmer gently for 45 minutes. Remove the parsley stalks and bay leaf.

To freeze:
Cool rapidly. Pour into suitable containers, allowing a 1-inch headspace. Cover and freeze.

To prepare for serving:
Reheat in a covered saucepan, over gentle heat.
Makes 4 pints.

Curry Sauce

3 tablespoons cooking oil
2 large onions, peeled and finely chopped
2 cloves garlic, *crushed with* 1 level teaspoon salt
3 tablespoons tomato purée
2 level tablespoons curry powder
2 level teaspoons curry paste
1 tablespoon brown sugar
2 tablespoons mango chutney, chopped
1 11-oz. can tomatoes
1 bay leaf
1 pint stock *or*
   stock and gravy, mixed

Heat the oil in a saucepan, add the onions and garlic and cook gently until soft but not until brown. Stir in the tomato purée, curry powder and curry paste, cook for 2 minutes. Add the remaining ingredients, cover with a lid and simmer for 45 minutes.

To freeze:
Cool and pack into ½-pint waxed cartons or polythene containers, leaving ½-inch headspace. Seal and freeze.

To prepare for serving:
Immerse in hot water to loosen the contents. Reheat gently in a saucepan. Use for curried eggs, chicken or vegetables. Makes approximately 1½-pints.

Onion Sauce

1 lb. onions, peeled and chopped
2 level tablespoons cornflour
½ pint milk
1 chicken stock cube

Put the onions in a saucepan, cover with water and bring slowly to the boil. Drain and return the onions to the pan, cover with fresh water, bring to the boil and simmer until tender. Drain and reserve ½-pint of the liquid.

In a mixing bowl, mix the cornflour with 3 tablespoons of the milk, to make a smooth paste. Combine the remaining milk with the onion water and bring to the boil. Meanwhile, stir in the crumbled stock cube.

Pour the boiling liquid on to the cornflour mixture, stirring all the time, return to the pan, add the onions and continue to cook for 2 minutes, stirring constantly. Cover the surface of the sauce with greaseproof paper and cool.

To freeze:
Pour into ¼-pint used cream cartons, polythene or waxed containers. Seal and freeze.

To prepare for serving:
Immerse the container in hot water to loosen the contents. Reheat gently.   Makes 1½-pints.

Bread Sauce
1½ pints milk
1 small onion, peeled and finely chopped
1 blade mace
6 white peppercorns
½ teaspoon salt
6 oz. breadcrumbs, freshly made
2 oz. butter

Heat the milk in a saucepan and add the onion, mace and peppercorns. Simmer for 30 minutes. Strain into a clean saucepan, add the salt, breadcrumbs and butter. Simmer gently until the sauce is of a thick, creamy consistency.

To freeze:
Cool and pack into used ¼-pint cream cartons or plastic containers, leaving ½-inch headspace. Seal with double thicknesses of foil.

To prepare for serving:
Immerse the carton in hot water to loosen the contents. Turn into a small pan and reheat over gentle heat. Add 1 tablespoon of cream before serving, if liked.   Makes 1½-pints.

Salmon Fish Cakes
3 7½-oz. cans salmon
3½ lb. potatoes, cooked and mashed
2 tablespoons chopped parsley, blanched
salt and pepper to taste
2 beaten eggs and breadcrumbs, for
    coating

Salmon Fish Cakes

Drain and flake the salmon, removing any skin and bones. Combine with the potatoes, parsley and seasoning. Divide the mixture in half and roll both pieces into sausage shapes. Cut each into 18 equal-sized pieces. Shape into cakes; dip in the beaten egg and coat with breadcrumbs.

To freeze:
Wrap the fish cakes, either in a double thickness of foil or in an air-tight container, with sheets of moisture-vapour-proof paper or foil between the layers. Seal and freeze.

To prepare for serving:
Heat fat in a frying pan. Shallow-fry the required number of unthawed fish cakes.
    Makes 3 servings for 4.

American Fish Pie

2½ lb. fresh cod or haddock, cooked
½ pint white sauce, coating consistency
1 oz. parsley, blanched and chopped
salt and pepper to taste
¼ level teaspoon nutmeg
juice of ½ lemon
3 lb. potatoes, mashed
1 lb. tomatoes, skinned and sliced
12 oz. cheese, grated

Remove skin and bones from fish, flake without mashing. Add to sauce with the parsley, seasonings and lemon juice.

To freeze:

Arrange alternate layers of mashed potatoes and fish, with a layer of tomatoes and cheese between them, in 3 foil pie dishes, loaf tins or other suitable containers. Finish with layers of mashed potato. Smooth the tops and seal with double thicknesses of foil.

To prepare for serving:

Uncover container and bake in centre of a hot oven, unthawed, (400 deg. F. – Gas Mark 6) for 40–45 minutes. Fork up the potato after the first 10 minutes of cooking time, to give a better appearance. Makes 3 servings for 4.

Fish Chowder

3 lb. smoked haddock
bouquet garni
1 thick slice lemon
2 pints water
1½ oz. butter
1 large onion, peeled and finely chopped
2 oz. cornflour
2 pints milk
2 teaspoons tomato purée *mixed with* juice ½ lemon
pinch pepper
¼ level teaspoon ground mace
6 oz. Patna rice, boiled

Rinse the haddock and cut into large pieces. Put it into a large saucepan. Place bouquet garni in the pan with the lemon slice and water. Bring to the boil, then lower the heat and simmer gently until the fish is cooked (approximately 15 minutes). Remove the bouquet garni and lemon slice, drain off the liquid and set aside. Cool the fish, remove the skin and bones then flake without mashing. Rinse the saucepan and melt the butter in it, add the onion and cook until soft but not brown. Blend the cornflour with ¼ pint of the milk; add to the pan with the remaining milk, reserved fish stock, tomato mixture, pepper and mace. Stir until boiling then reduce the heat and continue to cook for a further two or three minutes.

To freeze:

Cover the liquid in the pan with a buttered paper and allow to cool. Mix in the flaked fish and rice. Pack in polythene bags, plastic or other suitable containers, leaving a ½-inch headspace. Freeze.

To prepare for serving:

Thaw, overnight, in the refrigerator. Reheat gently in a saucepan. Sprinkle each serving with chopped parsley. Makes 3 servings for 4.

Beef Goulash

1½ oz. lard or dripping
3½ lb. stewing steak, trimmed and cut into 1-inch cubes
1 clove garlic
1 level teaspoon caraway seeds
1½ lb. onions, peeled and sliced
1 level tablespoon paprika pepper
1 11-oz. can tomatoes
1 level teaspoon sugar
salt and pepper to taste
¼ pint stock or water

Heat the lard in a large saucepan. Brown the meat, a third at a time, over a brisk heat. Crush the garlic with the caraway seeds and add to the pan with the onions, lower the heat and cook until the onions are soft. Add the remaining ingredients, cover with a lid and simmer very gently for 1¼ hours.

To freeze:

Cool rapidly and pack into foil or plastic containers *or* partially freeze in a covered, foil-lined meat tin, then cut into squares and wrap each portion in double thicknesses of foil. Return to the freezer.

To prepare for serving:
Thaw at room temperature for about 4 hours. Reheat in a saucepan. Add $\frac{1}{4}$ oz. *beurre manié* (see page 54) and cook for a further 2 minutes. Remove from the heat and add 3 tablespoons of yoghourt.   Makes 3 servings for 4.

Braised Steak with Mushrooms

Farmhouse Brisket
8 oz. streaky bacon, diced
4 lb. brisket, boned and rolled
1 lb. onions, sliced
1½ lb. carrots, sliced
3 sticks celery, cut into ½-inch pieces
1½ oz. plain flour
1½ pints brown ale
1 tablespoon brown sugar
1 teaspoon salt
pinch pepper
1 bay leaf

Fry the bacon gently, to render down the fat. Transfer to a casserole dish. Fry the meat, briskly, in the fat, turning to brown on all sides. Add to the bacon in the casserole.
Lower the heat under the frying pan, add the onions and fry gently until soft but not brown. Add the carrots and celery and cook for a further 5 minutes. Stir in the flour and cook for another 2 minutes.
Spoon the vegetables around the meat and add the remaining ingredients. Cover with a lid and cook in the centre of a warm oven (325 deg. F. – Gas Mark 3) for 2–2½ hours.

To freeze:
Cool and cut the meat into slices. Pack flat in 3 suitable foil or plastic containers, cover closely and freeze.

To prepare for serving:
Immerse the container in hot water to loosen the contents, transfer to a saucepan and reheat gently.   Makes 3 servings for 4.

Steak, Kidney and Mushrooms
3 lb. stewing steak, cut into 1-inch cubes
12 oz. ox kidney, cored and cubed
2 oz. flour, seasoned
2 oz. lard *or* dripping
2 large onions, peeled and sliced
12 oz. mushrooms, sliced
1½ pints chicken stock *or*
    2 stock cubes plus water

Toss steak and kidney in flour. Heat the fat in a frying pan. Add onions, fry gently for 5 minutes, transfer to a casserole dish. Put steak and kidney into pan and fry briskly to brown. Put into the casserole dish, add the mushrooms and stock. Cover with a lid and cook in a moderate oven (350 deg. F. – Gas Mark 4) for 1½ hours.

To freeze:
Cool rapidly and pack in 3 foil, plastic or other suitable containers, cover and freeze.

To prepare for serving:
Reheat without thawing, in a moderate oven or gently in a pan.   Makes 3 servings for 4.

Braised Steak with Mushrooms
2 oz. dripping *or* lard
3 lb. braising steak
1½ lb. onions, peeled and sliced
1½ lb. carrots, peeled and sliced
1 head celery, chopped
6 oz. mushrooms, sliced
½ bottle red cooking wine
1½ pints beef stock *or*
    2 stock cubes plus water
salt and pepper to taste

11

Heat dripping in a large pan, cut meat into ½-inch slices, fry briskly to seal on both sides. Remove and keep hot. Add onions, carrots, celery and mushrooms to pan and cook for 2 minutes. Put vegetables and meat into casserole. Add wine, stock and seasoning. Cover and cook in a moderately hot oven (375 deg. F. – Gas Mark 5) for 1½ hours.

To freeze:

Cool rapidly. Pack in 3 foil or plastic containers or in polythene bags. Seal and freeze.

To prepare for serving:

Remove from freezer 2 hours before use. Heat in a moderately hot oven (375 deg. F. – Gas Mark 5) for 35–40 minutes.

Makes 3 servings for 4.

Portuguese Cobbler

2 oz. dripping *or* lard
2 large onions, peeled and chopped
2½ lb. pie veal, cut into 2-inch cubes
2 oz. flour
2 15-oz. cans tomato soup
1 lb. carrots, peeled and sliced
salt and pepper
2 green peppers, de-seeded and diced
6 oz. mushrooms, sliced
For the topping:
12 oz. plain flour
6 level teaspoons baking powder
1 teaspoon salt
4 oz. margarine *or* lard
¼ pint plus 2–3 tablespoons milk

Melt fat in a 3½–4-pint flame-proof dish, fry onions and meat until lightly browned, remove them from the dish. Stir the flour into the fat, add the soup and bring to the boil. Return the onions and meat to the dish, add the carrots and season to taste. Cook in a slow oven (300 deg. F. – Gas Mark 2) for 2 hours. Add the green peppers and mushrooms 20 minutes before the end of the cooking time. Remove from the oven and turn the thermostat up to 425 deg. F. – Gas Mark 7. Sieve the flour, baking powder and salt into a mixing bowl. Rub in the fat and add sufficient milk to make a soft dough. Cut into 1½–2-inch circles,

place on a greased baking sheet and brush with milk.

Bake in the top of the pre-heated oven for 10–12 minutes. Cool on a wire rack.

To freeze:

Cool and pack the meat mixture in 3 foil pie dishes. Seal with double thicknesses of foil. Pack cobblers separately in polythene bags. Seal tightly and freeze.

To prepare for serving:

Place unthawed meat in pre-heated oven (325 deg. F. – Gas Mark 3) for about 1 hour. 10 minutes before the end of cooking time, remove the foil and arrange cobblers to cover surface of meat.   Makes 3 servings for 4.

Portuguese Cobbler

Osso Buco

6 lb. shin of veal, chopped in 2-inch pieces
2 oz. flour, seasoned
4 oz. butter or margarine
2 carrots, peeled and cut into thick slices
1 onion, peeled and sliced
1 clove garlic
1 level teaspoon salt
1 2¼-oz. can of tomato purée
¾ pint chicken stock *or*
    1 stock cube plus water
pinch pepper
1 bay leaf
1 teaspoon sugar

Coat the veal with seasoned flour. Melt the butter in a large frying pan and put the carrot and onion into the pan. Peel and crush the garlic with the salt and add it to the vegetables in the pan. Fry gently for 5 minutes. Transfer the vegetables to a large saucepan. Put the veal into the frying pan and brown on all sides, over strong heat. Transfer the meat to the saucepan and add the remaining ingredients. Cover with a lid and simmer gently for 2 hours. Strain the sauce and reserve.

To freeze:
Cool, discard the vegetables and bay leaf. Remove the meat from the bones. Pack the veal into 3 plastic, foil or other suitable containers. Divide the sauce between the 3 servings. Seal and freeze.

To prepare for serving:
Immerse the container in hot water to loosen the contents. Reheat in a covered saucepan over gentle heat.   Makes 3 servings for 4.

Country Braise
2 oz. lard *or* dripping
2 large onions, peeled and sliced
1 lb. carrots, peeled and sliced
1 large cooking apple, peeled, cored and
    sliced
3 lb. stewing veal, cut into 1-inch cubes
2 oz. flour, seasoned
¾ pint chicken stock *or*
    1 stock cube plus water
3 tablespoons tomato ketchup
4 oz. prunes, soaked for 2 hours and stoned
2 oz. almonds, blanched and chopped
Heat the lard in a large saucepan, add the onions, carrots and apples and fry until lightly

Country Braise

browned; remove from the pan. Toss veal in the flour and fry gently for 5 minutes. Return vegetables to the saucepan, add stock and tomato ketchup, bring to the boil then simmer very gently for 1 hour.

To freeze:
Cool, add prunes and almonds. Pack in 3 plastic containers or polythene bags, seal and freeze.

To prepare for serving:
Thaw at room temperature, allowing approximately 4 hours. Turn into a saucepan, bring to the boil, cover with a lid and simmer for 30 minutes.   Makes 3 servings for 4.

Devilled Rabbit
12 rabbit pieces
2 tablespoons malt vinegar
2 tablespoons mild mustard, freshly made
1 tablespoon curry powder
5 tablespoons corn oil
12 oz. pickled pork, diced
2 onions, peeled and chopped
seasoned flour, for coating
1½ pints chicken stock *or*
    2 stock cubes plus water
4 level tablespoons cornflour
6 tablespoons milk
salt and pepper to taste
1 teaspoon white vinegar
Put the rabbit pieces into a bowl of cold water, add 2 tablespoons vinegar and leave to soak for about 1 hour. Drain and pat dry. Mix the mustard and curry powder. Spread over the rabbit joints. Leave for another 30–40 minutes for the flavour to penetrate. Heat the oil in a heavy pan. Add the pork and the onion. Cook the onion until transparent but not brown. Dip the rabbit pieces into the flour; add them to the pan and brown lightly on all sides. Pour the stock over, and stir until boiling. Cover with a lid and simmer gently for 1 hour. Blend the cornflour with the milk and add to the pan. Remove from the heat, check the seasoning and add the white vinegar. Cool.

To freeze:
Pack into 3 foil-lined serving dishes. Cover with foil and partially freeze. Remove from the serving dishes, when sufficiently solid to do so,

13

and over-wrap with double or heavy duty foil. Seal and freeze.

To prepare for serving:

Unwrap and return to the original serving dish. Reheat in a hot oven (400 deg. F. – Gas Mark 6). Makes 3 servings for 4.

Liver and Onion Casserole

3 lb. ox liver, sliced and trimmed
2 oz. flour, seasoned
3 oz. dripping *or* lard
2 lb. onions, peeled and sliced
¾ pint beef stock *or*
   1 stock cube plus water
½ teaspoon mixed herbs

Soak the liver in cold, salted water for 30 minutes. Dry on absorbent paper then coat in the seasoned flour. Melt the fat in a heavy saucepan or flameproof casserole and cook the onion gently until soft but not brown. Remove onion and set aside. Fry the liver briskly in remaining fat to seal on both sides. Return onion to pan and add any remaining seasoned flour. Stir well, then add the stock and herbs. Cover casserole with a lid and cook in a warm oven (325 deg. F. – Gas Mark 3) for 1½ hours.

To freeze:

Cool rapidly. Spoon into 3 plastic or foil containers. Seal and freeze.

To prepare for serving:

Thaw overnight in the refrigerator. Reheat gently, in covered pan.

Makes 3 servings for 4.

Cutlet Turnovers

12 large lamb cutlets, boned
1½ lb. puff pastry
½ pint onion sauce (see page 18)

Trim the fat from the meat and roll tightly. Secure each with a cocktail stick. Grill and set aside to cool. Remove the cocktail sticks.

For ease of handling, cut the pastry into three equal pieces. Roll each piece into a 16-inch square, trim the edges and cut into quarters. Spoon a little sauce into the centre of each square and top with a lamb cutlet.

Damp two adjoining edges of each square and fold over to make a triangle. Seal and pinch the edges. Place in the refrigerator to chill the pastry thoroughly.

To freeze:

Pack upright, in a suitable polythene container or a biscuit tin, with foil or moisture-vapour-proof dividing papers between each. Seal and freeze.

To prepare for serving:

Place, unthawed, on a wet baking sheet. Brush with milk, cook in a very hot oven (450 deg. F. – Gas Mark 8) for 20 minutes. Makes 12.

Moussaka

2 oz. lard *or* dripping
1 large onion, peeled and finely chopped
3 lb. raw shoulder lamb, minced
salt and pepper to taste
3 tablespoons tomato purée
1 tablespoon sugar
3 large aubergines, sliced and sprinkled
   with salt
1 clove garlic, crushed
1 11-oz. can tomatoes
¾ pint cheese sauce
3 oz. cheese, grated

Heat 1 oz. of lard or dripping in a saucepan. Add the onion and allow to colour. Add the meat and stir over a brisk heat to brown. Season with salt and pepper, add tomato purée and sugar. Set aside. Wash the aubergines under cold, running water. Dry on kitchen paper. Heat the remaining fat in the pan, add two aubergines to the pan and cook for 5–7 minutes, add the garlic and tomatoes. Cover the pan and continue to cook for a further 5 minutes.

To freeze:

Divide the meat mixture between 3 foil dishes. Top with remaining aubergine and cheese sauce. Sprinkle 1 oz. cheese on each dish. Seal with double thicknesses of foil and freeze.

To prepare for serving:

Uncover, place in a hot oven (400 deg. F. – Gas Mark 6) for 40 minutes.

Makes 3 servings for 4.

Moussaka

Potted Hough
1½ lb. shin of beef
2–2½ lb. knuckle of veal, chopped by the butcher
1½ teaspoons salt
6 peppercorns
1 bay leaf

Put the beef, veal and salt into a large saucepan, add enough water to cover and bring to the boil. Simmer until the meat is tender (approximately 3 hours). Strain the liquid into a clean saucepan. Cool the meat, cut into small pieces and divide between 3 1-pint foil pudding basins.

Put the bones into the stock with the peppercorns and bay leaf. Boil rapidly, without a lid, to reduce to ½ pint. Strain the stock on to the meat and leave to set.

To freeze:
Cover the basins with double or heavy duty foil, seal and freeze.

To prepare for serving:
Thaw overnight in the refrigerator. Serve with salad.　　　Makes 3 servings for 4.

Terrine of Game
2 oz. butter
1 pheasant, plucked and drawn
2 partridges, plucked and drawn
12 oz. shin of veal, chopped into 2-inch pieces
3 pints stock or water
3 cloves
10 white peppercorns
2 teaspoons salt
¼ pint dry, white wine

Melt the butter in a large, heavy saucepan. Brown birds over a brisk heat. Put all the birds back into the pan with the veal, stock, cloves, peppercorns and salt. Bring to the boil; lower the heat, cover and simmer for 1½–2 hours. Remove the birds and the veal from the pan, cool and cut into pieces. Discard the bones. Strain the stock into a clean saucepan, add the wine and boil rapidly to reduce by two-thirds. Meanwhile, arrange the game in 3 foil-lined terrines or small pie dishes. Skim fat from stock and pour it over the game. (Older birds may be used for this dish.)

To freeze:
Cool rapidly, until set. Cover with foil and partially freeze. Remove from the terrine and over-wrap with a double or heavy duty foil. Return to the freezer.

To prepare for serving:
Thaw overnight in the refrigerator. Serve in the original dish.　　　Makes 3 servings for 4.

Beef Galantine
2 lb. rump steak
12 oz. cooked ham
1 large onion, peeled and quartered
1½ lb. tomatoes, skinned
6 oz. white breadcrumbs
2 eggs, lightly beaten
salt and pepper to taste

Cut away any fat or gristle from the steak and ham. Mince the steak, ham and onion finely, by passing it through the mincer two or three times. Blend or sieve the tomatoes and add to the meat mixture with the remaining ingredients. Mix thoroughly to combine.

Divide the mixture into three equal portions. Press each into a 1-pint foil basin. Cover with aluminium foil and steam gently for 3 hours.

Cool in the refrigerator or larder with a kitchen weight on each basin.

To freeze:
When quite cold, re-cover the dishes with foil and seal before freezing.

To prepare for serving:
Thaw overnight in the refrigerator or at room temperature for 4 hours.

　　　Makes 3 servings for 4.

15

Cornish Pasties

1½ lb. shortcrust pastry
For the filling:
1¼ lb. lean beefsteak
2 medium potatoes, diced
2 medium onions, peeled and finely chopped
2 tablespoons chopped, blanched parsley
salt and pepper to taste
1 tablespoon stock or water

Mince the meat finely and add to the other filling ingredients. Divide the pastry into 12 portions and roll each piece into a 5-inch circle. Put a spoonful of the filling into the centre of each piece of pastry, damp the edges, fold in half and seal. Flute the edges by pinching between the thumb and first two fingers. Stand the pastries upright on a greased baking sheet, brush with egg and milk and set aside in a cool place for 30 minutes, to allow the pastry to relax. Bake in the centre of a moderately hot oven (375 deg. F. – Gas Mark 5) for 35 minutes.

To freeze:
Allow to become completely cold. Pack in polythene, aluminium foil or other suitable containers, seal and freeze.

To prepare for serving:
Allow to thaw at room temperature for approximately 4 hours. Reheat in a cool oven.
Makes 3 servings for 4.

Devonshire Pasties

1 lb. shortcrust pastry
For the filling:
1 lb. raw beef, minced
12 oz. mushrooms, chopped
1 11-oz. can sweetcorn with peppers
salt and pepper
beaten egg

Mix minced meat, mushrooms and drained sweetcorn and season with salt and pepper. Roll out pastry to about ⅛-inch thick and cut into circles around a saucer. Divide the filling evenly between the pasties, damp the edges with water, fold over and seal. Brush with beaten egg and make a couple of slashes on top of each pasty. Bake in a hot oven (425 deg. F – Gas Mark 7) for about 30 minutes, when the pastry should be crisp and golden.

To freeze:
Allow to become completely cold. Pack into a suitable container, cover closely and freeze.

To prepare for serving:
Reheat frozen pasties in a moderate oven (350 deg. F. – Gas Mark 4), for approximately 20 minutes.
Makes 3 servings for 4.

Chicken Special

2 medium-sized chickens
3 pints water
1 lb. streaky bacon
1 lb. button mushrooms
3 oz. butter
3 oz. flour
salt and pepper to taste

Simmer the chickens in the water until tender. Set aside until cool. Reserve stock for sauce. Chop the bacon into 2-inch pieces after removing the rind. Cut mushrooms in half. Fry the bacon until crisp and remove from the pan. Cook the mushrooms gently in the bacon fat. Melt the butter in a clean saucepan, add flour and cook for 1 minute. Season to taste, remove from heat and gradually stir in 1½ pints stock. Return to heat and bring to boil, stirring. Remove all the flesh from the chickens and cut into bite-size pieces; add to the sauce with the bacon and mushrooms.

To freeze:
Cool rapidly, pack in foil, plastic or other suitable containers. Seal tightly and freeze.

To prepare for serving:
Immerse the container in hot water to loosen the contents. Turn into a saucepan and reheat gently. Add a small packet of frozen peas and continue to cook for a further 7 minutes.

Makes 3 servings for 4.

Creamed Pimento Chicken Pie
6 oz. butter
5 oz. flour
salt and pepper to taste
2 pints chicken stock *or*
   2 stock cubes plus water
1 pint milk
2½ lb. cooked chicken, chopped
1 small can pimento
For the pastry crust
1 lb. flaky pastry

Melt the butter over low heat, blend in the flour smoothly and the seasonings. Gradually stir in the chicken stock and the milk. Bring to the boil, stirring constantly, allow to boil for 1 minute. Stir in the chicken, and the finely chopped pimento together with the liquid from the can. Cool and pack into 3 foil pie dishes.

To make the crust, divide pastry into 3, roll out thinly and use to cover the pies. Dampen edges and decorate without breaking the seal. Pierce a hole in the centre and bake in a hot oven (425 deg. F. – Gas Mark 7) for 15 minutes. If necessary, reduce heat slightly and continue cooking for another 5–10 minutes or until golden brown.

To freeze:
Wrap each pie separately in double or heavy duty foil. Seal tightly and freeze.

To prepare for serving:
Thaw in refrigerator and reheat in a moderately hot oven (375 deg. F. – Gas Mark 5) for about 1 hour.

Note: The pies can be frozen with the pastry unbaked, after sealing the edges of the crusts. Do not pierce a hole in the pastry. Place unbaked in freezer to harden the pastry, then wrap in foil. Freeze.

                  Makes 3 servings for 4.

Scalloped Turkey with Rice
8 oz. Patna rice
3 oz. butter *or* margarine
1 lb. mushrooms
3 oz. flour
salt and pepper to taste
¾ pint hot milk
1 pint hot chicken stock
2½ lb. cooked turkey, chopped
1 medium green pepper, de-seeded

Cook the rice in plenty of boiling salted water until just tender. Drain and rinse in a colander, using fresh, hot water. Melt 1 oz. of the butter and fry the mushrooms for 1 minute only. Remove from the pan, add rest of butter and make a thick sauce with the flour, seasoning, milk and stock. Stir constantly over moderate heat until sauce is smooth and thick.

To freeze:
Pack in foil dishes or other suitable containers, with layers of rice, mushrooms and turkey. Pour one third of the sauce into each container. Chop pepper finely and sprinkle evenly over the three containers. Cool quickly. Cover closely with foil.

To prepare for serving:
Put into the top of a moderately hot oven (375 deg. F. – Gas Mark 5), turning frequently to heat right through.   Makes 3 servings for 4.

Note: Cooked rice frozen this way defrosts well.

Cider Gammon with Apples
12 slices gammon
black pepper to taste
6 oz. butter
1½ pints cider
12 oz. button onions
8 sticks celery
9 tomatoes, quartered
12 oz. mushrooms
6 dessert apples, cored and sliced
3 oz. flour

Place the gammon in a casserole, sprinkle in the pepper. Add half the butter and 2 tablespoons of the cider. Cover with a lid and bake in a moderately hot oven (375 deg. F. – Gas Mark 5) for 15–20 minutes. Meanwhile melt the remaining butter and fry all the vegetables and the apples in it. Add the flour and cook, stirring, for a few minutes. Gradually pour in the cider, and stir until smooth. Pour over the gammon, re-cover the casserole and continue cooking in the oven for a further 20 minutes.

To freeze:
Cool rapidly, put into 3 suitable containers, cover closely and seal before freezing.
To prepare for serving:
Thaw at room temperature for about 6 hours. Reheat in a covered casserole in a moderately hot oven. Stir in ¼ pint single cream just before serving.　　　　　Makes 3 servings for 4.

Cider gammon with apples (recipe page 17)

Steak and Kidney Pudding
For the pastry:
1 lb. self-raising flour
2 teaspoons salt
pinch pepper
8 oz. shredded beef suet
cold water to mix
For the filling:
2 lb. stewing steak, cut in 1-inch cubes
8 oz. ox kidney, cored and cut in pieces
1 oz. flour, seasoned
6 tablespoons water

Sift together flour and salt. Add suet and add enough water to make a firm dough. Cut off ⅓ of the pastry and divide the remaining pastry into 3. Use these pieces to line 3 1½-pint greased pudding basins.

Toss meat in seasoned flour and divide between basins. Pour 2 tablespoons water into each basin. Damp edges of pastry and top basins with remaining pastry, rolled into circles. Cover with greased foil and steam for 3 hours.

To freeze:
Cool quickly. Put into a polythene bag. Seal and freeze.

To prepare for serving:
Remove polythene bag and thaw at room temperature for 6–8 hours. Steam for 1½ hours.
　　　　　Makes 3 servings for 4.

Variations
Rabbit and Bacon Pudding
Omit steak and kidney and use 2 lb. jointed rabbit, blanched, 1 lb. lean collar bacon, soaked and cut in cubes, 2 large onions, sliced, 4 oz. mushrooms, chopped, 2 cooking apples, peeled, cored and chopped and 1 teaspoon dried sage.

Veal, Gammon and Mushroom Pudding
Omit steak and kidney and use 2 lb. pie veal, cut in 1-inch cubes, 12 oz. lean gammon, cut into ½-inch pieces, 8 oz. mushrooms, chopped, grated rind 1 lemon and ¼ teaspoon dried thyme.

Rhubarb and Orange Pudding
Omit steak, kidney, flour and water and use 2 lb. rhubarb, cut in 1-inch pieces, grated rind and chopped segments of 2 large oranges and 6–8 oz. sugar. Steam for 2 hours only before freezing.

Gooseberry Pudding
Omit steak, kidney, flour and water and use 2 lb. gooseberries, topped and tailed and 6–8 oz. sugar. Steam for 2 hours only before freezing.

Plum and Apple Pudding
Omit steak, kidney, flour and water, and use 2 lb. plums, halved and stoned, 2 cooking apples, peeled, cored and sliced and 8 oz. sugar. Steam for 2 hours only before freezing.

Steamed Syrup Pudding
3 rounded tablespoons golden syrup
12 oz. self-raising flour
4 level teaspoons baking powder
1 level teaspoon mixed spice
½ level teaspoon salt
8 oz. luxury margarine
8 oz. castor sugar
4 large eggs
3 tablespoons milk

Put a tablespoon of syrup into each of 3 1-pint foil pudding basins. Sieve flour, baking powder, mixed spice and salt into a mixing bowl. Add remaining ingredients, beat for 2 minutes or until all the ingredients are blended. Spoon equal quantities of the mixture into the pudding basins. Seal the tops of the basins with foil and steam for 1½ hours.

To freeze:
Cool, re-seal with double or heavy duty foil.

To prepare for serving:
Steam pudding for approximately 30 minutes, or until hot.   Makes 3 servings for 4.

Peel, halve and core the pears, place at once into the warm syrup

Pears in spiced honey syrup
6 oz. clear honey
1½ pints water
3 oz. crystallised ginger, sliced
good pinch cinnamon
6 tablespoons lemon juice
3 lb. dessert pears, not quite ripe.

Use a wide shallow pan which will allow the pears to lie in a single layer or cook the pears a few at a time. Put the honey and water in the pan and stir over a gentle heat until the honey dissolves. Add the sliced ginger, cinnamon and lemon juice. Peel and halve the pears. Remove cores and put immediately into the syrup. The pears must be kept covered with syrup throughout cooking and freezing to avoid discoloration. Poach them gently until they are tender.

To freeze:
Stand the pan in cold water to cool them quickly. Arrange pears carefully in plastic containers leaving ¾-inch headspace, cover with syrup, then place crumpled foil on top of the fruit to keep it submerged. Cover closely and freeze.

To prepare for serving:
Thaw at room temperature and serve while the fruit is still chilled. Decorate with piped whipped cream and a sprinkling of cinnamon.
                    Makes 3 servings for 4.

Arrange pears carefully into rigid containers leaving a good headspace and fill with sufficient syrup to cover

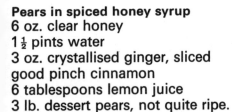

Place crumpled foil over the pears to keep them submerged

Pears in spiced honey syrup, delicious served with whipped cream and cinnamon

19

Butterscotch Sauce

6 tablespoons golden syrup
2 oz. brown sugar
1 oz. butter
$\frac{3}{4}$ pint water
1 tablespoon custard powder, *mixed with juice of 1$\frac{1}{2}$ lemons*

Melt the syrup, brown sugar and butter in a heavy saucepan, heat gently to combine. Remove from heat and add the water, pour over the custard mixture and return to the saucepan. Stir over gentle heat until thickened.

To freeze:
Cool and pack into $\frac{1}{4}$-pint waxed cartons or plastic containers. Seal and freeze.

To prepare for serving:
Immerse the container in hot water. Put the contents into a saucepan and heat gently. Serve hot with ice cream.   Makes $\frac{3}{4}$-pint.

Raspberry Sauce

1 lb. raspberry jam
juice 2 lemons
$\frac{1}{2}$ pint water
2 level tablespoons arrowroot

Combine the jam, lemon juice and water in a saucepan. Blend the arrowroot with some of the liquid, bring the remainder to the boil and add the blended arrowroot. Cook for a further 2 minutes stirring constantly. Strain to remove the pips.

To freeze:
Cool and pack into $\frac{1}{4}$-pint waxed cartons or plastic containers. Seal and freeze.

To prepare for serving:
Immerse the container in hot water. Turn out into a saucepan and simmer gently.
                                Makes 1-pint.

Apricot Oat Crumble

1 lb. dried apricots, soaked and stewed
2 oz. plain flour
4 oz. butter, melted
6 oz. demerara sugar
8 oz. rolled oats

Divide the fruit into three portions and spread into the bases of 3 1-pint foil dishes. Mix the flour, butter and sugar into the rolled oats and scatter over the top of the fruit.

To freeze:
Seal with double thicknesses of foil and freeze.

To prepare for serving:
Remove the cover and sprinkle the surface of the crumble with sugar. Bake in a moderate oven (350 deg. F. – Gas Mark 4), without thawing, for 40 minutes.

                        Makes 3 servings for 4.

Fruit Creams

$\frac{1}{2}$ pint fruit purée
$\frac{1}{2}$ pint custard (made with 2 tablespoons custard powder)
2 level tablespoons powdered gelatine
$\frac{1}{4}$ pint warm water *or* fruit juice
$\frac{1}{2}$ pint evaporated milk, scalded
juice of 1 lemon
castor sugar to taste

Combine the fruit purée and custard. Dissolve the gelatine in the water. Whisk the evaporated milk and fold it into the fruit, with the lemon juice and sugar. Add the dissolved gelatine to the mixture and whisk until setting.

To freeze:
Pour into 3 plastic, foil or other suitable containers. Seal and freeze.

To prepare for serving:
Remove the lid and thaw at room temperature for approximately 4 hours.

                        Makes 3 servings for 4.

Traditional Trifle

8 individual sponge cakes, crumbled
6 tablespoons sherry
6 tablespoons raspberry jam
12 macaroons
2 oz. flaked almonds
$\frac{3}{4}$ pint cold custard

Divide the cake crumbs and press into the bases of 12 individual foil pie plates. Sprinkle with sherry and top with raspberry jam.

Sprinkle with crumbled macaroons and flaked almonds; and top with custard.

To freeze:
Seal the dishes with double or heavy duty foil and freeze.

To prepare for serving:
Thaw, covered at room temperature for about 2 hours. Decorate with whipped cream.

Makes 3 servings for 4.

Raisin Ice Cream
1 14-oz. and 1 6-oz. can evaporated milk, chilled
3 oz. castor sugar
juice of 2 lemons
6 oz. seedless raisins
½ teaspoon vanilla essence
1 level tablespoon gelatine
3 tablespoons warm water

Whisk all the evaporated milk until thick. Beat in the sugar, lemon juice, raisins and vanilla essence. Dissolve the gelatine in water in a small saucepan. Heat gently, but do not allow to boil.

Quickly stir into the evaporated milk and whisk until on the point of setting. Pour into a polythene container, cover with a lid and freeze for two hours. Whisk the mixture to break down the ice particles, cover and return to the freezer.

Makes 3 servings for 4.

White Bread
Dry mix:
1 lb. plain flour
2 level teaspoons salt
½ oz. lard rubbed into flour
Yeast liquid:
Mix ½ oz. fresh yeast in ½ pint water *or* dissolve 1 teaspoon sugar in ½ pint warm (110 deg. F.) water, sprinkle on 2 level teaspoons dried yeast. Leave until frothy (about 10 minutes).

Mix dry ingredients with yeast liquid using a wooden fork or spoon, then work with one hand to a firm dough adding extra flour, if needed, until dough leaves sides of the bowl clean. Turn on to a lightly floured board and knead thoroughly to stretch and develop dough. To do this fold dough towards you, then push down and away with palm of hand. Repeat for about 10 minutes until dough feels firm and elastic and no longer sticky. After kneading, shape dough into a ball. Place in a large, lightly greased polythene bag.

To freeze unrisen dough:
Seal bag tightly and place in freezer.
Note: If dough might rise slightly before freezing, leave 1-inch space above dough.

To freeze risen dough:
Loosely tie bag, leaving room for dough to rise. Allow to rise until double in size:
Quick rise: 45–60 minutes in a warm place.
Slower rise: 2 hours average room temperature.
Overnight rise: up to 12 hours in a cold larder or refrigerator.

Risen dough springs back when pressed with a lightly floured finger. Turn risen dough on to a lightly floured board and flatten firmly with the knuckles to knock out air bubbles, then knead until firm. Place in lightly greased polythene bag, tightly seal and place in freezer.

To prepare unrisen dough for use:
Thaw, about 5–6 hours at room temperature, then leave to rise and knock back, as above.

To prepare risen dough for use:
Thaw about 5–6 hours at room temperature.

To shape the dough:
For tin loaves, divide dough into the quantity required (i.e., leave whole for a large loaf, or divide into two for two small loaves) and shape the loaves as follows. Flatten dough with the knuckles to an oblong the width of the tin. Fold in three and turn over so that seam is underneath. Smooth over the top and tuck in the ends. The loaves are now ready to rise again (this is known as proving). Put tins inside a greased polythene bag and leave until dough rises to tops of tins. This takes 30–40 minutes at room temperature, or leave in a refrigerator if a slow rising is more convenient. Remove from polythene bag and bake loaves in centre of a very hot oven (450 deg. F. – Gas Mark 8) for 30–40 minutes or until loaves shrink slightly from sides of tins and sound hollow when tapped on base, cool on a wire tray.

Chapter Two
Chain cooking

Minced meat shaped into patties.
Packed in plastic containers, with
dividing papers between each layer.

Steak Maison

Planning ahead can save you a great deal of time and effort, as well as money. We've seen how this applies to cooking main dishes in large quantities, so that you can serve one meal at once, and freeze the rest. But if the freezer is used really intelligently, this kind of planning can be carried even further.

At the time of year when a seasonal glut makes apples cheap, for instance, buy a really large quantity. One afternoon's work in the kitchen will keep you supplied for many months to come with apple purée for pies and other sweets, apple sauce for meat dishes, fresh sliced apples for cooking as well as using in salads, when this most popular of all fruits is scarce and expensive.

You may notice a special offer of chicken at a lower-than-usual price, either by your usual frozen food supplier, or at a local supermarket. Sometimes one shop brings down the price of chicken to a level that is not really economic, but which tempts many extra customers to do a week's shopping for groceries there, instead of at their usual stores. When chicken is a 'loss leader', as it's called, rush in and take advantage of the bargain. This is the time to go in for chain cooking. Buy a dozen roasters, and a few hours work will provide you with plenty of frozen pieces ready to cook, various prepared chicken dishes that only need thawing and reheating, and lots of good strong stock made from the carcasses.

It may be that you just happen to have some time to spare. No food is specially cheap, but you do have free time and stove space for a big cook-up. A large quantity of minced beef, always a good economy buy for main meal dishes, can be made up into a variety of dishes and sauces. Again, a few hours spent cooking ahead, will save you many chores in the months to come.

MINCED BEEF CHAIN
Make up 7 lb. of the basic recipe, then by making simple additions you can produce five different dishes – amounting to 40 servings.

Basic Meat Recipe
2 oz. dripping *or* lard
2 lb. onions, peeled and chopped
3 cloves garlic, crushed
7 lb. minced beef
1 2¼-oz. can tomato purée
2 level tablespoons sugar
2 level teaspoons salt
½ level teaspoon pepper

Heat the fat in a very large saucepan or a preserving pan, then fry the onion and garlic over gentle heat until soft but not brown. Add the meat and fry briskly, stirring constantly to brown. Mix in the remaining ingredients and remove from the heat.

Steak Maison

2 lb. basic meat recipe
2 green peppers, de-seeded and chopped
4 tablespoons tomato ketchup
1 level teaspoon salt
2 16-oz. cans baked beans in tomato sauce

Combine the meat, peppers, ketchup and salt in a saucepan. Cover with a lid and simmer over a low heat for 30 minutes. Add the baked beans.

To freeze:
Cool rapidly. Line a meat tin with aluminium foil. Pour the mixture into the tin, cover with foil then partially freeze. Remove from the tin and cut into portions. Quickly re-wrap in double or heavy duty foil and return to the freezer.

To prepare for serving:
Unwrap the required number of portions. Re-heat in a casserole in the oven or in a tightly covered saucepan.   Makes 2 servings for 4.

Baboti

1 slice bread, 1½ inches thick
½ pint milk
2 lb. basic meat recipe
1 tablespoon Worcestershire sauce
3 level tablespoons curry powder

Trim the crusts from the bread, cut into cubes and soak in the milk for 10 minutes. Mix with meat, Worcestershire sauce and curry powder.

To freeze:
Pack into foil dishes without pressing the mixture down. Seal with double or heavy duty foil and freeze.

To prepare for serving:
Thaw in the refrigerator, overnight. Uncover and pour a lightly whisked egg over the meat. Cook in a moderate oven (350 deg. F. – Gas Mark 4) for approximately 40 minutes.
      Makes 2 servings for 4.

Shepherd's Pie

2 lb. basic meat recipe
1 level tablespoon curry powder
2 oz. flour
2 tablespoons brown table sauce
¾ pint stock *or*
    1 stock cube plus water
3 lb. mashed potato
salt and pepper to taste

Put the meat into a saucepan and stir in the curry powder, flour and sauce. Cook over gentle heat, stirring constantly, for 5 minutes. Add the stock, bring to the boil and cover with a tight-fitting lid. Simmer gently for 20 minutes.

To freeze:
Cool rapidly. Fill aluminium pie dishes or loaf tins two-thirds full. Cover with lightly seasoned mashed potato. Then smooth the tops and seal with double or heavy duty foil and freeze.

To prepare for serving:
Remove the foil cover. Reheat in the top of a fairly hot oven (400 deg. F. – Gas Mark 6) for 30–40 minutes. Remember to fork up the potato after the first 10 minutes of cooking.
      Makes 2 servings for 4.

Chilli con Carne

1½-2 lb. basic meat mixture
2 level teaspoons chilli powder
2 16-oz. cans baked beans
1 11-oz. can tomatoes

Combine all the ingredients in a saucepan. Cover with a lid and simmer gently for 40 minutes.

To freeze and prepare for serving:
Follow the instructions for Steak Maison.
      Makes 2 servings for 4.

Bolognaise Sauce

1 lb. basic meat recipe
1 11-oz. can tomatoes
¾ pint stock *or*
    1 stock cube plus water
¼ pint red cooking wine (optional)

Combine all the ingredients in a pan. Cover with a tight-fitting lid, simmer gently for about 1 hour.

To freeze:
Cool rapidly. Pour into used cream cartons or plastic containers, leaving ½-inch headspace. Seal and freeze.

To prepare for serving:
Immerse the container in hot water for a few minutes, to loosen the sauce. Turn into a saucepan, cover with a lid and bring to boiling point.
      Makes 2 servings for 4.

Chicken Turnovers; Vol-au-vent filling; Kromeskies; and Stuffed Pancakes.

Chicken pieces, plain and coated

CHICKEN CHAIN

The recipes in this section show just how versatile chicken can be. Buy a dozen roasters at a time and use them in the following way. Freeze two whole.

For Chicken Kiev use:

❋ The breasts and wings of three chickens.

For Chicken Pieces use:

❋ The remainder of the three chickens, plus an additional one, cut into joints, making 12 pieces in all. Egg and breadcrumb six and leave the others plain. Wrap in double foil or moisture-vapour-proof paper, or place in foil dishes and seal with double thicknesses of foil.

For Chicken Curry use:

❋ Two chickens jointed into 12 portions.

For Chickenburgers use:

❋ The meat from two boned chickens.

For Chicken Turnovers, Kromeskies, Vol-au-vents, and stuffed Pancakes use:

❋ Three chickens, roasted.

For Chicken Stock use:

❋ All the carcasses.

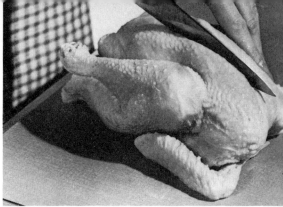

Thaw bird sufficiently to remove giblets from body cavity. Place on chopping board and with sharp knife cut through and along length of breastbone.

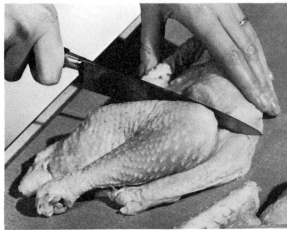

Lay halves of chicken skin side up on board and divide each in half again by cutting diagonally across between wing and thigh. Bird is now in four quarters.

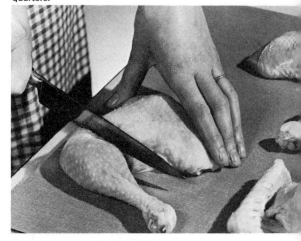

To make six joints divide each thigh and drumstick portion in half by cutting through at ball and socket joint.

Open bird out, then cut through along length of backbone. If liked, backbone can be removed entirely by cutting along close to either side. Tap back of knife sharply with heavy weight to cut bird in half through bony sections.

Here are the four quarters: two wing and breast joints, two thigh and drumstick joints. Joints are neater if leg shanks and wing tips are removed as shown.

Chicken Curry
12 chicken pieces
seasoned flour, for coating
2 oz. lard *or* dripping
8 oz. onion, peeled and chopped
1 pint curry sauce (see page 8)

Coat the chicken pieces in the seasoned flour. Melt the fat in a large, heavy frying pan; add the onion and cook until transparent. Transfer to a baking dish. Add the chicken pieces, a few at a time, to the fat in the pan and cook until brown on all sides.

Place the chicken in the dish with the onion, add sauce, cover with foil. Bake in a moderate oven (350 deg. F. – Gas Mark 4) for 1 hour.

To freeze:
Cool rapidly and pack into suitable containers.

To prepare for serving:
Reheat, unthawed, in a saucepan. Serve with plain boiled rice.   Makes 12 portions.

Chickenburgers
3 slices white bread
1 lb. shoulder of veal, skinned
1 3-lb. chicken, boned
$\frac{1}{4}$ pint milk
$\frac{1}{2}$ teaspoon salt
$\frac{1}{4}$ teaspoon nutmeg
1 large egg

Soak the bread in the milk. Trim veal and cut chicken into pieces. Mince meats finely. Mix in the bread and all remaining ingredients. Divide into 12 portions and shape into patties.

To freeze:
Wrap in double or heavy duty foil. Use dividers between the layers if to be stacked. Seal and freeze.

To prepare for serving:
Shallow-fry thawed or frozen, in plenty of butter or oil.   Makes 12.

Chicken Turnovers
12 oz. puff pastry
12 oz. cooked chicken, finely chopped
1 small onion, finely chopped
1 10$\frac{1}{2}$-oz. can condensed mushroom soup
1 tablespoon chopped parsley, blanched
$\frac{1}{2}$ teaspoon salt
dash of Worcestershire sauce

Roll the pastry to $\frac{1}{8}$-inch thickness. Cut into 5-inch circles, using a saucer. Combine remaining ingredients and put a spoonful of filling into centre of each pastry circle. Damp edges and seal with the prongs of a fork.

To freeze:
Pack into foil or plastic containers. Cover closely and seal before freezing.

To prepare for serving:
Put the turnovers, unthawed, on a wet baking sheet, brush with beaten egg and cook in a very hot oven (450 deg. F. – Gas Mark 8) for 30 minutes.   Makes 12.

25

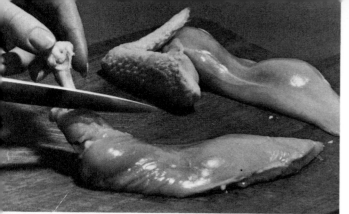
Scrape the meat back from the bone.

Place a portion of butter in the centre of each chicken breast, and then roll it.

Dip in beaten egg and coat with crumbs.

Chicken Kiev—see recipe below.

Chicken Kiev

3 whole chicken breasts, with wings
    attached
6 oz. parsley butter
salt and pepper to taste
seasoned flour
1 egg, lightly beaten
toasted breadcrumbs for coating

To remove the chicken breasts:

Skin the chicken and place with the front facing you. Using a sharp filleting knife, carefully remove the flesh from one side of the breast bone, without piercing the meat. Gradually work the tip of the knife down towards the wing. Sever the tendon between the ball and socket wing-joint and cut through the skin underneath it. Repeat this process on the other side of the chicken. Treat the two other chickens in the same way. Cut off the two end bones from each wing, scrape back meat from remaining bone (see pictures, page 26).

Put each chicken breast between two sheets of wet greaseproof paper and pound until thin, taking care not to split the meat. Roll the butter, cut into 6 equal portions and place one in the centre of each breast.

Sprinkle with salt and pepper. Roll up envelope fashion, letting the wing bone protrude. Toss each roll in well-seasoned flour; dip into the egg and coat with crumbs.

To freeze:

Pack in a plastic container, cover closely and freeze.

To prepare for serving:

Thaw overnight in the refrigerator. Deep fry in hot oil, drain and serve. Garnish with parsley, and top with a little extra parsley butter if liked.

Serves 6.

Illustrated in colour on the front cover.

Kromeskies

1 lb. cooked chicken
8 oz. cooked ham or bacon
3 oz. margarine
1 large onion, peeled and finely chopped
1 clove garlic, crushed
3 oz. flour
¾ pint chicken stock or
    1 stock cube plus water
2 tablespoons tomato ketchup
salt and pepper to taste
¼ level teaspoon powdered mace
12 rashers streaky bacon, trimmed

Put the chicken and ham through a fine mincer. Melt the margarine in a saucepan and add the onion and garlic. Cook gently until soft but not brown. Stir in the flour and cook for 1 minute, gradually add the stock. Add all the other ingredients, with the exception of the bacon. Bring to the boil and cook gently, beating with a wooden spoon, until the mixture begins to leave the sides of the pan. Spread into a sandwich tin and leave to cool. Meanwhile, stretch the bacon by smoothing it with a dinner knife and cut each rasher in half. When the mixture is quite cold, divide it into 24 equal portions. Flour both hands and roll each portion into a ball and then into a cork shape. Wrap a piece of bacon around each kromesky.

To freeze:

Arrange in oblong plastic or foil containers. Stack layers on top of each other, with foil or moisture-vapour-proof paper dividers between. Seal and freeze.

To prepare for serving:

Thaw at room temperature, allowing approximately 2 hours. Toss in seasoned flour, dip in coating batter and deep-fry in hot fat (380 deg. F.) for 2–3 minutes.   Makes 3 servings for 4.

Chicken Stock

To each pound of chicken bones and trimmings use:

3 pints water
1 small carrot, sliced
1 small onion, stuck with a clove
a small bouquet garni

Wash the carcasses and trimmings. Place in a large saucepan and add the water. Bring slowly to the boil and simmer for 2 hours. Skim frequently to remove the fat from the surface of the stock and the sides of the pan. Add the remaining ingredients and enough cold water, to replace that which has evaporated. Simmer gently for one more hour. Skim again and strain the stock through a muslin cloth.

Put the stock into a clean pan; add the vegetables and bouquet garni. Return to the boil and simmer for another 30 minutes. Remove any remaining scum with kitchen paper.

To freeze:

Cool and pack into plastic containers or polythene bags leaving a 1-inch headspace. Separate cubes, frozen in an ice cube tray from the refrigerator, supply just enough strong stock to improve a gravy or sauce.

To prepare for serving:

Heat in a saucepan and use as a base for soups or sauces.

Vol-au-vent Filling

1½ pints milk
1 small onion
blade of mace
4 oz. butter or margarine
3 oz. flour
salt and pepper to taste
1 green pepper, de-seeded
8 oz. button mushrooms, quartered
1¼ lb. cooked chicken, diced

Warm the milk with the onion and mace. Allow to infuse for 30 minutes, then strain. Melt 3 oz. of the butter in a saucepan; stir in the flour and cook gently for a further 2 minutes. Draw the pan off the heat and whisk in the milk. Blanch the green pepper in boiling water for 7 minutes. Immerse in cold water to cool. Cut into ¼-inch dice.

Heat the remaining butter in a small saucepan; add the pepper and mushrooms and cook for 1½ minutes. Add, together with the chicken, to the sauce. Return the pan to the heat, bring to the boil and cook for a further 2 minutes, stirring continuously. Season to taste.

To freeze:
Cool rapidly and pack into a large plastic bowl if required for a forthcoming party, or pack it into several small containers if the filling is required for family meals.

To prepare for serving:
Thaw either in the refrigerator or at room temperature. Time required depends on size of container. Reheat in a saucepan before filling the vol-au-vent cases. Fills 12 large cases.

Chicken Pancakes
For the filling:
2 oz. butter
1 large onion, peeled and finely chopped
2 oz. flour
1 pint chicken stock or milk
1 lb. cooked chicken, finely minced
salt and pepper to taste
dash Worcestershire sauce
36 small thin pancakes
1 pint tomato sauce (see page 8)
12 oz. cheese, grated

Melt the butter in a saucepan, add the onion and cook until soft. Gradually stir in the flour and cook gently for 2 minutes, add the stock or milk, bring to the boil and cook for a further 2 minutes, stirring constantly. Stir in the remaining ingredients. Allow the mixture to cool, then spoon a little of the filling into each pancake. Roll and pack closely in foil-lined dishes. Cover with tomato sauce (see page 00), sprinkle with grated cheese.

To freeze:
Cover with foil and partially freeze. When the pancakes are sufficiently solid, lift out of the dishes and wrap in double or heavy duty foil. Seal and return to the freezer.

To prepare for serving:
Unwrap and return the pancakes to their original dishes. Thaw at room temperature allowing approximately 5 hours. Cook in a moderately hot oven (375 deg. F. – Gas Mark 5) for 30–40 minutes. Makes 3–4 servings for 4.

APPLE CHAIN
Buy 16 lb. of cooking apples. If they are slightly damaged, buy a few extra pounds and discard the bruised parts. Use 8 lb. for the Basic Apple Purée recipe, then pack in ¼- or ½-pint containers. These small packs can be thawed quickly without waste for use in puddings, sauces or as baby food.

Use the remainder of the apples, sliced. A few can be stored with blackberries – by the dry pack method – for pies or to serve as stewed fruit. Store some slices in plain syrup packs and some unsweetened, but for convenience store the largest portion in dry sugar packs. Use these for puddings and pies.

Basic Apple Purée Recipe
8 lb. cooking apples
½ pint water
2 oz. butter or margarine
juice and zest of a lemon
8 oz. granulated sugar

Wash and quarter the apples. Put them into a large saucepan or preserving pan without peeling or coring. Add the water, butter or margarine, lemon juice and zest. Cover with a lid or piece of aluminium foil. Cook gently, shaking the pan from time to time. When the apples are almost pulped add the sugar and then beat with a wooden spoon until completely smooth. Continue to cook until the sugar is completely dissolved. Rub the mixture through a fine hair or nylon sieve and discard the peel and cores.

To freeze:
Pour the purée into cream cartons, plastic or other suitable containers, leaving ½-inch headspace. For convenience, pack in small quantities, just enough for one serving or to suit your family's needs. Seal and freeze.

To prepare for serving:
Either thaw at room temperature (the amount of time required depends on the size and shape of the container) *or* place the container under hot, running water to loosen. Turn the contents into a saucepan and thaw by heating.

Apple Purée

Apple Slices

Apple Snow

Recipes using apple purée
Apple Snow
sugar to taste
½ pint basic apple purée recipe, thawed
green colouring
2 egg whites

Add the sugar to the apple purée and tint with a little green colouring but be careful not to add too much. Whisk the egg whites stiffly and fold into the apples. Spoon into individual dishes and chill; and, if liked, garnish with apple slices before serving.　　　　　　　　Serves 4.
Illustrated in colour on the back cover.

Apple Fool
¼ pint custard, cold
½ pint basic apple purée, thawed
sugar to taste

Mix the custard into the apple purée. Sweeten to taste and spoon into individual dishes. Chill before serving.　　　　　　　　　　Serves 4.

Baked Apple Soufflé
3 oz. castor sugar
pinch ground cinnamon
½ pint basic apple purée, thawed
2 large eggs, separated

Mix the sugar and cinnamon into the apple purée then beat in the egg yolks. Whisk the egg whites stiffly and fold into the mixture using a metal spoon. Spoon into a heavily greased 1½-pint soufflé or pie dish. Bake in the centre of a moderate oven (350 deg. F. – Gas Mark 4) for 30–40 minutes or until firm to touch and golden brown. Serve at once with cream or custard.　　　　　　Serves 4.

Apple Cheese Flan
6 oz. shortcrust pastry
2 eggs, lightly whisked
3 oz. castor sugar
finely grated rind of ½ lemon
¼ pint basic apple purée, thawed

Line an 8-inch flan or loose-based sandwich tin with the pastry. Prick the base and bake blind, in a pre-heated hot oven (400 deg. F. – Gas Mark 6) for 15 minutes. Meanwhile, beat the eggs, sugar and lemon rind into the apple purée.

Remove the flan from the oven and lower the heat to 350 deg. F. – Gas Mark 4. Pour the filling into the case. Continue to cook for 30–35 minutes or until the filling is firm. Serve hot or cold.　　　　　　　　　Serves 6.

29

Apple Slices

Peel, core and cut 8 lb. apples into $\frac{1}{2}$-inch slices. Blanch in boiling water for 1 minute, and pack into polythene bags or other suitable containers. Seal and freeze.

To prepare for serving:
Partially thaw in sealed container, at room temperature.

Recipes using apple slices
Apple Charlotte
12 oz. apple slices, partially thawed
3 oz. breadcrumbs
1 oz. brown sugar
1 tablespoon golden syrup
grated rind and juice of $\frac{1}{2}$ lemon
Grease a $\frac{3}{4}$-pint pie dish and arrange the apple slices and breadcrumbs in alternate layers, starting and finishing with breadcrumbs.
Warm the remaining ingredients in a small saucepan, to blend. Spoon syrup over crumbs. Bake in the centre of a warm oven (325 deg. F. – Gas Mark 3) for 50–60 minutes. Garnish with grated lemon rind.   Serves 4.
Illustrated in colour on the back cover.

Apple Pancakes
4 oz. plain flour
pinch salt
1 egg
$\frac{1}{2}$ pint milk
oil, for greasing pan
3 oz. castor sugar
$\frac{1}{2}$ pint water
8 oz. frozen apple slices, partially thawed
Sieve the flour and salt into a mixing bowl, make a well in the centre and break in the egg. Add 4 tablespoons of the milk and stir to a smooth paste. Whisk in the remainder of the milk – the surface should be covered with tiny bubbles.
Grease the base of a 7-inch omelet pan and heat. Add a little batter at a time and cook on both sides. When all the pancakes are cooked, set aside to keep hot.
Dissolve the sugar in the water and boil rapidly for 5 minutes, lower the heat and add the

Apple Charlotte

partially thawed apple slices, simmer gently until tender. Drain and spoon into the centre of each pancake. Roll the pancakes up and place them on a serving dish.   Makes 12.

Eve's Pudding
12 oz. apple slices, partially thawed
3 oz. castor sugar
4 oz. plain flour
$1\frac{1}{2}$ level teaspoons baking powder
pinch salt
2 oz. margarine
1 egg
$\frac{1}{4}$ teaspoon vanilla essence
2–3 tablespoons milk
Mix the apple slices with 1 oz. of the castor sugar and arrange them in a 1-pint pie dish. Sieve flour, baking powder and salt. Add remaining sugar and fat, cut into pieces, to the flour. Rub in until the mixture resembles fine breadcrumbs. Beat egg lightly with the vanilla essence. Mix into the fat and flour with sufficient milk to make a creamy consistency.
Spread mixture over surface of apples and bake in a moderate oven (350 deg. F. – Gas Mark 4) for 40 minutes.   Serves 4.

Apple Pie
8 oz. shortcrust pastry
12 oz. apple slices, partially thawed
2 oz. castor sugar
3 whole cloves
To decorate:
beaten egg white *or* milk
castor sugar

30

Divide the pastry into two pieces, one slightly smaller than the other. Knead each to a smooth ball. Roll the smaller piece very thinly, to fit an 8–8½-inch pie plate. Cover the plate with the pastry and press out all the air bubbles, starting from the centre.

Put a thick layer of apple over the pastry; sprinkle with castor sugar and add the cloves. Pile the remaining apple slices on top and smooth to a flat dome. Damp edges of pastry. Roll remaining pastry and, without stretching it, cover top of pie. Press the edges together to seal; trim and flute. Make a small vent in the centre, brush with milk or lightly beaten egg white and sprinkle with castor sugar. Bake in centre of a moderate oven (350 deg. F. – Gas Mark 4) for 30–40 minutes.　　Serves 4.

Apple and Sultana Layer Pudding
3 oz. self-raising flour
pinch salt
¼ level teaspoon mixed spice
1½ oz. white breadcrumbs
2 oz. shredded suet
3–4 tablespoons milk
For the filling:
8 oz. apple slices, partially thawed
2 oz. sultanas
2 oz. brown sugar
rind of ½ lemon, finely grated

Sieve the flour, salt and mixed spice into a mixing bowl. Stir in the breadcrumbs and suet. Add sufficient milk to make a soft, scone-like dough. Divide into three unequal portions. Prepare the filling by finely chopping the apple slices. Mix with the remaining ingredients. Grease a 1-pint pudding basin and pat out the smallest piece of suet pastry to fit the base of the bowl. Add half the fruit filling and pat out the second piece of pastry to cover this. Add the rest of the filling and pat out the remaining pastry to cover it. Cover the basin with a piece of foil. Steam for 1½–1¾ hours. Serve with custard.　　Serves 4.

Stewed Blackberry and Apple
2 oz. granulated sugar
¼ pint water
1½ lb. blackberry and apple,
　　partially thawed

Put the sugar and water into a saucepan. Dissolve the sugar over a gentle heat. Add the fruit and allow to simmer gently, covered with a lid, until tender. If the fruit overcooks it will break up and eventually turn to pulp. Serve hot or cold with cream or custard.　　Serves 4.

Chapter Three
Buffet parties

This kind of party has long been popular as the relaxed, easy way to entertain. The guests do most of the work once the party has started, helping themselves to plates, cutlery and food. However, it does pre-suppose that the hostess has lots of time on her hands for preparing the food beforehand.

You, the fortunate freezer owner, can spend an hour or two on several different days making up the provisions for the buffet table! You can also serve a frozen sweet straight from the freezer to add a dramatic touch to the festivities when the more solid titbits have disappeared and appetites are flagging. How else could you produce 15 or 20 frozen Orange Cups, each nestling in the skin of the orange and gleaming with frost, whenever you want to? The quantities given for recipes in the following section are for 15, as this is a fair average number for such a party.

If you are serving 15 guests, a selection of seven recipes should be adequate in quantity – two sweet, four cold savoury and one hot savoury should be an ideal balance of dishes. For fewer numbers, drop one savoury recipe, and for more, increase the selection, bearing in mind that most guests will average seven selections from the buffet table. (Greedy guests will eat more, but then there may be a few who will be too busy talking to eat as many.)

Another advantage which the freezer bestows is that you can prepare more than you think you will need and only completely thaw sufficient to set a generous table at the start of the party. If the food vanishes more rapidly than you had expected, you produce your extra supplies from the refrigerator. But if they are not needed, they can remain happily in the freezer for another day.

Onion Bread Rolls
½ pint tepid water
½ oz. dried yeast
1 level teaspoon sugar
2 tablespoons corn oil
1 lb. plain flour
1 packet French onion soup

Pour the water on to the yeast. Add the sugar and leave until the yeast has dissolved. Stir in the corn oil and mix well. Sieve flour into a mixing bowl and add the contents of the packet of soup. Stir in the liquid and mix to form a soft dough, adding a little more water if necessary. Beat the dough until it leaves the sides of the bowl clean. Cover with a damp cloth and leave to rise in a warm place, until double in bulk. Turn out and knead lightly.

Divide the dough into 15 equal portions and shape into rolls. Place on a greased baking sheet and leave to prove in a warm place for 10–15 minutes. Bake in a hot oven (425 deg. F. – Gas Mark 7) for 10–15 minutes.

To freeze:
Cool and pack in polythene bags. Seal tightly and freeze.

To prepare for serving:
Thaw at room temperature in the sealed bag.
Makes 15.

Hamburger Patties
2 lb. lean chuck steak
1 onion, peeled
1 clove garlic
2 slices bread
1 egg
1 teaspoon salt
pinch pepper
¼ level teaspoon sage

Remove all fat from steak, mince it twice with the onion and garlic, using coarse cutter. At the end of the second mincing, add the bread, so that this goes through the mincer last. Turn meat into basin, add beaten egg and seasoning. Mix well. Form into cakes about 3 inches across and $\frac{1}{4}$ inch thick.

To freeze:
Arrange four patties in a row, put a dividing piece of foil on top; continue to stack with foil dividers between each layer. Wrap tightly in double thicknesses of foil, seal and freeze.

To prepare for serving:
Partially thaw in the refrigerator, allowing 5 hours. Pat dry mustard into surface before grilling. Baste well with barbecue sauce while cooking. Sandwich hot patties between halves of soft rolls with more mustard and any good pickles, relishes, or thin slices of onion.
Makes 16–18 patties.

Savoury Sandwich Loaf
1 large white loaf, unsliced
2 eggs, hard-boiled
$\frac{1}{4}$ pint single cream
2 oz. butter
salt and pepper
squeeze of lemon juice
green colouring
1 tablespoon spinach purée
1 2-oz. jar lobster paste
3 packets demi-sel cheese

Remove the outside crust from the bread and then slice lengthways into four. Using a fork, mash the hard-boiled eggs, while still warm, with 1 tablespoon of the cream and $\frac{1}{2}$ oz. of the butter. Season well. Beat the remaining butter with a squeeze of lemon juice to soften and add a little green colouring. Add the spinach purée. Spread the first piece of bread with the lobster paste, and cover with second piece. Spread with the egg mixture, and cover with the third layer. Spread this one with the spinach butter and cover with the top layer of bread. Blend together the demi-sel cheese and the remaining cream until soft and of a spreading consistency. Completely cover the loaf with the cream cheese mixture and smooth with a palate knife. Chill and cut into slices, using a sharp knife. Reshape into a loaf.

To freeze:
Pack in a biscuit tin, or suitable plastic container. Seal and freeze.

To prepare for serving:
Thaw, covered, at room temperature, allowing approximately 5 hours. Cut each slice in half lengthways.
Makes 15 slices.

Sausage Rolls
2 7-oz. packets puff pastry
12 oz. pork or beef sausage meat
salt and pepper

Roll one packet of pastry thinly to approximately 12×6 inches. Trim edges with a knife and cut in half lengthways. Season the sausage meat well, divide in half and roll one portion into two long rolls the same length as the pastry. Place down the centre of each strip. Brush one side of the pastry with a little water, fold over and seal. Cut each strip, with a sharp knife, into 6 sausage rolls. Make up the other packet of pastry and the remaining sausage meat in the same way.

To freeze:
Chill until the pastry is firm. Stack in layers, with foil or moisture-vapour-proof dividing papers. Seal and freeze.

To prepare for serving:
Place frozen sausage rolls on wet baking sheets. Cook in a very hot oven (450 deg. F. – Gas Mark 8) for 10 minutes. Reduce the temperature to 425 deg. F. – Gas Mark 7 for a further 10 minutes.
Makes 24.

Cheese and Apple Horns
1½ lb. shortcrust pastry, *flavoured with*
   1 oz. Parmesan cheese, grated
1 egg, beaten
1 oz. extra Parmesan cheese, grated

Roll pastry to an oblong and trim $14 \times 4\frac{1}{2}$ inches, then cut into six strips each $\frac{3}{4}$ inch wide. Wind overlapping around horn tins. Place on a baking sheet, with the pastry ends underneath. Brush with egg, sprinkle with the extra Parmesan cheese. Bake in a fairly hot oven (400 deg. F. – Gas Mark 6) for 15–20 minutes. Cool on a wire tray.

To freeze:
Pack in a large plastic container or biscuit tin. Seal and freeze.

To prepare for serving:
Thaw, covered, at room temperature allowing approximately 5 hours. Fill with grated apple and cream cheese.　　　　Makes 18–20.

Cheese and Apple Horns

Tuna Mousse

Tuna Pâté

Tuna Mousse

3 7-oz. cans tuna steak
approximately ¾ pint milk
3 oz. butter or margarine
3 oz. flour
salt and pepper, to taste
4 eggs, separated
1 level tablespoon gelatine, *dissolved in*
　　4 tablespoons water
¼ pint double cream
¼ pint single cream
5 tablespoons tomato ketchup
1½ teaspoons anchovy essence
juice ½ lemon

Drain the liquor from the tuna and make up to 1½ pints with milk. Remove the skin and bones from the fish and mash with a fork until smooth. Melt the butter in a saucepan, stir in the flour and cook for 2 minutes. Gradually add the milk mixture, bring to the boil and cook for a further 2 minutes, stirring continuously to make a smooth sauce. Season, cool and beat in the egg yolks. Melt the gelatine in a small saucepan, but do not allow to boil. Whip the double and single cream together, until stiff enough to leave a trail. Add the gelatine, ketchup, anchovy essence and lemon juice to the sauce. Lightly fold in the whipped cream and stiffly beaten egg whites with a metal spoon. Pour into 3 1½-pint moulds.

To freeze:
Seal with double-thickness foil and freeze.

To prepare for serving:
Thaw overnight in the refrigerator. Unmould on to a serving dish. Decorate with lemon slices, olives and parsley.　　Serves 15.

Tuna Pâté

2 7-oz. cans tuna steak
little milk
blade mace
small piece bay leaf
sprig of parsley

34

black peppercorns
  oz. butter
 oz. flour
 tablespoons single cream or top milk
—2 teaspoons lemon juice
 few gherkins, finely chopped (optional)

Drain the liquor from the tuna and make up to
 pint with milk. Place in a saucepan with the
mace, bay leaf, sprig parsley and peppercorns.
Leave over a gentle heat to infuse for 15 minutes, bring to the boil, strain. Melt butter in a
small saucepan, and stir in the flour, cook
for 2–3 minutes, add the milk mixture and bring
to the boil, stirring, cook for 2 minutes. Mash
the tuna fish with a fork and add to the sauce
with cream, lemon juice, and gherkins, mix
well together. Add additional seasoning if
necessary. Place in a foil-lined serving dish
and leave in a cool place to set.

To freeze:
Cover with foil and partially freeze. When
sufficiently solid, remove from the container
and over-wrap with double or heavy duty foil.

To prepare for serving:
Unwrap and return to the original serving
dish. Thaw at room temperature allowing
approximately 2 hours. Decorate with parsley
and lemon. Serves 16.

Rice Salad
1 ½ lb. Patna rice
2 teaspoons salt
juice of a lemon
¼ pint olive oil
5 tablespoons tarragon vinegar
½ teaspoon grated nutmeg
⅛ teaspoon pepper
1 teaspoon castor sugar
2 green peppers, de-seeded and thinly
  sliced

Cook the rice for 15 minutes in plenty of fast-
boiling, salted water with the lemon juice
added to it. Wash the cooked rice under cold
water, drain, then dry in a warm oven. Whisk
the oil, vinegar, nutmeg, pepper and sugar
together. Add the green peppers to the rice and
toss both in the prepared dressing.

To freeze:
Pack into plastic or waxed containers, seal
and freeze.

To prepare for serving:
Thaw at room temperature. (The amount of
time required depends on the sizes of the containers.) Arrange slices of tomato around the
edge of the serving dish to make a garnish.
Serve with an assortment of cold meats.
Serves 15.

Kidney Risotto
3 tablespoons cooking oil
2 large onions, peeled and thinly sliced
2 cloves garlic, *crushed with*
  2 level teaspoons salt
2 lb. Patna rice
3 pints chicken stock *or*
  3 stock cubes plus water
3 green peppers, de-seeded and sliced
2 oz. butter
8 lambs' kidneys, trimmed and sliced
12 oz. mushrooms, quartered

Heat the oil in a large saucepan, add the
onions and garlic and cook over low heat until
soft but not brown. Add the rice and fry for
two minutes before adding the stock. Bring
to the boil, cover with a lid and simmer, very
gently, for 10 minutes. Add the peppers and
cook for a further 10 minutes. Heat the
butter in a frying pan and gently sauté the
kidneys; remove from the pan and replace
with the mushrooms, cook for 2 minutes.

To freeze:
Cool all the ingredients, then toss the kidneys
and mushrooms in the rice. Spoon into large
plastic containers or polythene bags, seal and
freeze.

To prepare for serving:
Immerse containers in hot water to loosen
the contents. Turn into meat dishes, cover
with foil and reheat in a warm oven (325 deg.
F. – Gas Mark 3). Place in serving dishes and
sprinkle with grated cheese. Serves 15.

Bring sun-drenched Italy into your home at any time of the year, with the aroma of delicious Italian cooking. Prepare enough Lasagne for several meals (recipe begins on this page), and arrange in foil trays.

The trays can either be frozen as they are, or with one tray up-turned on to the other (if you up-turn trays, only one need be foil covered).

With two trays up-turned one on the other, seal the joining edges with freezer tape. Don't use ordinary adhesive tape because it doesn't stand up to low temperatures.

As you go round the edge with the tape, pinch the trays together to make sure the tape adheres properly ensuring a good seal.

Barbecued Rice

2½ pints barbecue sauce, frozen(see
    page 8)
1 lb. Patna rice
2 12-oz. cans sweet corn, drained
3 green peppers, chopped
¼ teaspoon dried thyme
2½ pints tomato juice
15 slices processed cheese

Put frozen barbecue sauce in a shallow pan and add all remaining ingredients except cheese. Stir lightly to mix. Cover and simmer for 4 minutes, or until rice is tender. Stir and arrange cheese slices on top. Cover and cook until cheese starts to melt. Serve very hot. Serves 15.

Lasagne

1 2-lb. 3 oz. can tomatoes
1 pint tomato sauce (see page 8 for recipe)
1 teaspoon salt
¼ teaspoon pepper
4 tablespoons oil
2 large onions, sliced
1 clove garlic, crushed
2 lb. minced beef
2 1-lb. packets lasagne
3 8-oz. cartons cottage cheese
4 oz. Parmesan cheese, grated

Combine the tomatoes, tomato sauce, salt and pepper in a saucepan. Bring to simmering point and cover with a lid. Heat 3 tablespoons of the oil in a frying pan, add the onion and garlic and cook until soft but not brown. Stir the meat into the onion and cook briskly to brown. Spoon the meat into the tomato sauce and simmer, uncovered, for 1 hour. Add the remaining oil to a large saucepan (or preserving pan) of salted, boiling water. Add the lasagne and cook, at boiling point, for 12 minutes. Drain and separate the pieces.

To freeze:

Use foil dishes or line serving dishes with foil, spoon a little meat sauce into the base of each. Divide the cottage cheese, allowing equal proportions for each dish. Arrange alternate layers of lasagne, cottage cheese and sauce, finishing with the sauce. Sprinkle the top of each with grated cheese. Cover with foil and partially freeze. Remove from the containers and re-wrap in double or heavy duty foil. Return to the freezer.

To prepare for serving:

Remove the foil and transfer to the original serving dishes. Thaw at room temperature. Cook in a moderate oven (350 deg. F. – Gas Mark 4) for 30–40 minutes.   Serves 15.

Party Tartlets

Bake blind, your usual rich shortcrust pastry tartlet cases. When cold, stack them together, place them in suitable containers, seal, label and freeze.

When you are ready to use them, remove from the freezer and allow them to come to room temperature before crisping a little in the oven. Now add a hot savoury or sweet filling.

Raw pastry tartlet cases can be kept equally well in the freezer and are simply baked when required. However, for a party you will save a little time by baking them before freezing.

Small fruit tartlets are also excellent for buffet parties. Instead of a rich shortcrust pastry, use a biscuit crust mixture to make them more unusual.

Here is a good basic savoury filling:

1 oz. butter
1 level tablespoon flour
¼ pint chicken stock
2–3 oz. button mushrooms, washed but
    unpeeled
small nut butter
1 tablespoon water
1 teaspoon lemon juice
6 oz. cooked chicken or turkey, cut finely
2 tablespoons cooked peas
1 4½-oz. can pimento, cut in thin strips
    1 inch long and drained

Melt butter, stir in the flour to make a smooth *roux*. Remove from the heat and stir in

chicken stock and cook for a few minutes. Meanwhile, slice the mushrooms and cook them, covered, in a little butter, water and lemon juice. Add mushrooms to the sauce together with the chicken or turkey. Add peas and pimento. Heat through. Fill tartlet cases straight away and serve while still hot.

This filling can be made in advance and freezes well. When you are ready to use it, allow to thaw and then heat through before filling the warmed tartlet cases.

The basic savoury mixture can be varied in several ways. For instance, instead of chicken or turkey, use shelled shrimps or a can of crab meat, flaked, or tuna, or salmon. Or, if you have any cooked salmon in the freezer, flake it roughly and use as the basis of the recipe.

Apple Strudel

For the pastry:
8 oz. plain flour
½ level teaspoon salt
1 tablespoon beaten egg
1 teaspoon salad oil
¼ pint water
icing sugar

For the filling:
6 oz. demerara sugar
½ level teaspoon mixed spice
1 oz. sultanas
2 rounded tablespoons breadcrumbs,
    browned
1½ lb. frozen apple slices, partially thawed
2 oz. butter, melted

Sieve the flour and salt into a bowl and mix to a soft dough with the egg, oil and water. Throw the dough firmly on to a floured board, lift it with a twist of the wrist, then throw it down again. Repeat this for two or three minutes until the dough is pliable and smooth, and no longer sticks to the board. Then leave it in a floured bowl for at least 15 minutes.

Meanwhile, prepare the filling. Mix the sugar, mixed spice, dried fruit, and browned breadcrumbs together and add the apple slices. When the strudel dough has rested for 15 minutes roll it out on a floured board into a rectangle about 10×12 inches, keeping the shape as regular as possible. Lay an old clean tablecloth on the table, folded in half. Sprinkle it with flour, then place the rectangle of strudel paste in the centre. Then put your hands on the centre of the dough, palms downwards, and stretch out the paste gently. Continue stretching the paste evenly in this way, working from the centre, until it is almost transparent and measures about 36×18 inches.

Pull off any thick pieces of paste from round the edge and brush the entire surface lightly with three-quarters of the butter. Sprinkle the filling over the surface to within 1 inch of the edge. Roll up the strudel by lifting one end of the cloth and allowing the strudel to roll itself. Slip the rolled-up strudel on to an up-turned greased baking tray, form it into an 'S' shape, and brush with the remaining butter.

Bake the strudel just above the centre of a very hot oven (450 deg. F. – Gas Mark 8), for 10 minutes, then reduce the heat to 400 deg. F. – Gas Mark 6 for a further 20–30 minutes. When it is cooked, sprinkle the strudel with a little icing sugar rubbed through a rounded strainer.

To freeze :

Cut into 15 slices, pack into plastic containers, biscuit tins or cake boxes overwrapped with polythene.

To prepare for serving :

Thaw at room temperature for approximately 1 hour. Sieve icing sugar on the top and serve with fresh cream. Makes 15 slices.

Orange Cups
3 lemons
10 oranges, halved
water
1 lb. granulated sugar
4 egg whites

Pare the skin off 1 lemon and 5 orange halves. Squeeze and reserve the juice out of all the oranges and lemons, taking care not to split the orange cases. Set 15 orange halves aside. Add water to the fruit juice to make $2\frac{1}{2}$ pints and place in a large saucepan with the pared skin. Dissolve the sugar in the liquid over gentle heat. Bring to the boil and continue to boil rapidly without stirring, for 12 minutes. Cool and strain into a large mixing bowl. Freeze for 6 hours. To prepare the orange cases: insert the handle of a teaspoon between the pith and skin of each orange. Loosen the pith all the way round each case. Discard the pith. Break the prepared sorbet into pieces with a fork, and then mash. Whisk the egg whites stiffly and fold into the sorbet. Spoon into the prepared cases and return to the freezer with the remaining sorbet. Top each orange case with a scoop of the remaining sorbet before serving. Serves 15.

Pear Héléne Tartlets
3 oz. castor sugar
$\frac{1}{2}$ pint water
4 pears, peeled, cored and cut into quarters
juice $\frac{1}{2}$ lemon
8 oz. plain chocolate, melted
1 tablespoon oil
ice cream, for filling
15 frozen tartlet cases, thawed

Dissolve the sugar in the water, bring to the boil and continue to boil rapidly for 5 minutes. Lower the heat and simmer the pears in the syrup until tender, do not allow them to break. Drain, cool and sprinkle with lemon juice.

Add the oil to the melted chocolate and keep it warm.

Just before serving, put a scoop of ice cream in each case, top with a piece of pear and drizzle melted chocolate over. Makes 15.

Chapter Four
Teatime entertaining

Unexpected guests have an uncanny knack of dropping in for tea on the one day when you have nothing in the biscuit tin, and no freshly baked cakes to offer them. Such problems can be solved triumphantly with some short-term items from the freezer.

By this I mean such things as scones and tea breads, which you would not expect to keep frozen long, because they are rather bulky and have a relatively short freezer life. Cooked scones, for instance, should not be stored for more than two months, and uncooked biscuit dough for more than one month.

A basic biscuit mix can be flavoured in various ways, and each flavour stored in a Swiss roll shape, from which you cut slices of just the right thickness and bake them almost while the kettle boils. It would be worthwhile to double the quantities of the basic mix when making either, and cook a batch for instant eating and a batch to store.

Certain cakes freeze well, and all the recipes given here are freezer-tested for their qualities in retaining a 'good as new' flavour and texture when thawed after a month or more of storage.

If your home baked cakes appear, after freezing, to have a poor texture or flavour, this may be due to the choice of ingredients rather than to a fault in baking. Freshly bought flour should always be used as stale flour tends to deteriorate rapidly after freezing. Another factor which helps to retain the fresh flavour of the cake is the freshness of the fat used. Fats such as butter and margarine easily pick up cross-flavours from other foods if stored in the larder or refrigerator or simply left on an open dish in the kitchen. Eggs used in cakes for freezing ought always to be perfectly fresh and very well beaten.

Again, they must be extra fresh to avoid that disappointing 'flatness' of flavour when the cake is thawed out. The beating must be thorough because egg whites freeze more quickly than yolks and traces of unblended egg white will give the cake an uneven texture after thawing.

If you have time, make up a few fancy sandwiches as well as the standard meal size kind, and these will add an elegant touch to a tea-party table, or will add grace to a buffet spread. They store well for several weeks.

Here's how to make dainty pinwheel sandwiches for tea parties. Cut a sandwich loaf, lengthwise, into thin slices and remove the crusts. Spread each slice with different coloured suitable fillings and roll up tightly as for a Swiss roll, but *lengthwise*. Give the first roll a sharp press into shape; this is needed to make the final neat circle of each sandwich.

To freeze:
Wrap the rolls individually in waxed paper and slide them into a polythene bag, excluding as much air as possible. Fasten the end securely. These pinwheel sandwiches are now ready for a party, or (if frozen) for any time you may need them during the next few weeks.

To prepare for serving:
Remove the pinwheels from the freezer an hour or two before they are to be cut. Unwrap each roll, and place it join side down on a bread board. Cut into $\frac{1}{4}$-inch slices with a really sharp knife.

Sandwich fillings
Cream cheese with sweet pickles
Cream cheese with chopped chicken and grated lemon rind
Cream cheese with chopped salami sausage
Cream cheese and chopped dates
Peanut butter, cream cheese and chives

Blue cheese, chopped bacon and Chilli sauce

Cheddar cheese, grated, with chopped olives

Cream cheese and chopped olives

Sliced ham, tongue or corned beef with finely minced onion

Cream cheese and liver pâté with Worcestershire sauce

Chopped chicken, ham and almonds

Chopped cooked liver, crisp bacon and pickles

Chopped frankfurters and Chilli sauce

Chopped prawns, cream cheese and lemon juice

Chopped prawns, cottage cheese and sweet pickles

Flavoured Butters for Pinwheel Sandwiches

As these sandwiches look much prettier if the filling contrasts well in colour with the bread, the best method is to blend the filling with the butter for spreading so that you can see what the colour of the finished sandwiches will be.

Green butter Cream 4 oz. of butter, work in 1 heaped tablespoon of very finely chopped parsley, the juice of ½ lemon, salt and pepper to taste.

Anchovy butter Cream 4 oz. of butter, work in 4 chopped and pounded anchovy fillets, a pinch of pepper and a few drops of pink food colouring.

Mustard butter Cream 4 oz. of butter, work in a level dessertspoon of French mustard.

Shrimp butter Cream 2 oz. butter with a small carton of potted shrimps (including their own butter).

Ginger Danish Pastries

½ oz. yeast

1¾ oz. castor sugar

8–12 tablespoons tepid milk

12 oz. plain flour

pinch salt

7 oz. butter

Filling A:

2 oz. ground almonds *mixed with*
   5 pieces chopped stem ginger and
   2 tablespoons ginger syrup

Ginger Danish Pastries

Filling B:

2 oz. ground almonds

5 pieces stem ginger, chopped

Cream the yeast with 1 teaspoonful of sugar. Pour ¼ pint of the tepid milk into the yeast. Sift the flour and salt into a bowl, add the remaining sugar. Make a well in the centre and pour in the yeast mixture. Work into the flour adding the remaining milk if necessary, to form a light but dry dough. Knead until smooth.

Roll into an oblong ½ inch thick and place knobs of butter, the size of walnuts, over two-thirds of the surface. Fold and roll as for rough puff pastry and repeat once. Wrap in grease-proof paper and place in a refrigerator or cool place for 15 minutes, or until firm. Repeat the rolling and folding until all the butter is worked in. Chill for 1 hour or overnight. When firm, roll out into a square ¼ inch thick. Cut in half.

Spread one half with the ground almond filling A. Roll up into a sausage shape and cut into six pieces. Cut each slice twice, two-thirds of the way down and fan out. Cut the other half into squares. Fill half the squares with chopped ginger and nuts (Filling B) and fold the corners to the centre. Make the rest of the pastry and filling into your favourite shapes. Place on greased baking sheets, covered, in a warm place to prove for 10–15 minutes. When the pastries have increased their size by half, glaze with beaten egg white. Place in a hot oven (450 deg. F. – Gas Mark 8) for 15–20 minutes until golden brown. Cool on a wire tray.

To freeze:

Seal tightly in polythene bags.

To prepare for use:
Thaw at room temperature allowing approximately 2 hours. Makes about 15 pastries.

Pork Pie for High Tea
For the pastry
4 oz. plain flour
½ level teaspoon salt
1½ oz. white fat or lard
2 tablespoons water
For the filling
12 oz. pork sausage meat
pinch powdered sage
salt and pepper to taste

Combine sausage meat, sage, salt and pepper, then mix thoroughly to make sure seasonings are well mingled, set aside until pastry has been made.

Sieve the flour and salt into a warm bowl. Measure the fat and water into a small saucepan and bring to a rolling boil. Pour immediately into the centre of the flour and mix to a smooth ball with a wooden spoon. Turn on to a board and knead until smooth. Reserving a little for the lid and decoration, shape the remainder into a round. Flatten the base and begin to shape the sides. Place the sausage meat in the centre and gradually work the pastry up round the side to form an edge. Roll reserved pieces out to form a lid. Damp the edge of the pie with a little beaten egg and milk, and place the lid over the top. Pinch the edges to seal and snip round with scissors. Flute the edges of the pie. Make a hole in the centre and decorate with leaves made from any remaining pastry. Brush with beaten egg and fix a greased band of paper around the pie. Place pie in the centre of a very hot oven (425 deg. F. – Gas Mark 7) for 20 minutes, then lower the heat to 350 deg. F. – Gas Mark 4 and bake for a further 40 minutes. After 30 minutes remove the band of paper and brush the whole pie with beaten egg.

To freeze:
Allow to become completely cold. Wrap in a double thickness of foil and seal well.

To prepare for serving:
Thaw at room temperature allowing at least 8 hours. Serves 6.

Basic Biscuit Dough
1 lb. plain flour *and*
  1 level teaspoon baking powder
8 oz. butter or margarine
8 oz. castor sugar
2 eggs, beaten
½ teaspoon vanilla essence
little milk
½ teaspoon coffee essence

Sieve the flour and baking powder on to a piece of paper. Cream together butter and sugar until light and fluffy. Add the beaten eggs, a little at a time, alternately with a few spoonfuls of sifted flour. Mix in the rest of the flour. Divide mixture in half. Add vanilla essence to one half and work it into the dough with sufficient milk to make a firm paste. Add coffee flavouring to the other half of the mixture and work into dough in the same way.

To freeze:
Form each portion into a roll, and wrap in moisture-vapour-proof paper or aluminium foil. Seal and freeze.

To prepare for serving:
Thaw at room temperature until the roll is soft enough to slice into ¼-inch slices and bake in a moderately hot oven (375 deg. F. – Gas Mark 5) for 10–15 minutes. If liked decorate by lightly pressing a glacé cherry or almond in the centre.

One Stage Peanut Cookies
6 oz. plain flour
½ level teaspoon baking powder
¾ level teaspoon bicarbonate of soda
¼ level teaspoon salt
4 oz. luxury margarine
3 tablespoons peanut butter
3 oz. castor sugar
3 oz. soft brown sugar
1 standard egg

Sieve the flour, baking powder, bicarbonate of soda and salt into a mixing bowl. Place the remaining ingredients in the bowl and beat together with a wooden spoon until well mixed (approximately 2–3 minutes). Gather the mixture together with the fingertips and form into a roll.

To freeze:
Cut the roll into 4 pieces and place dividing papers between them. Wrap the rolls in moisture-vapour-proof paper or aluminium foil. If wrapped in moisture-vapour-proof paper, seal before freezing.

To prepare for cooking:
Unwrap and thaw at room temperature until the dough is soft enough to slice. Cut thinly and place fairly wide apart, on a greased baking sheet. Bake in the centre of a moderately hot oven (375 deg. F. – Gas Mark 5) for 7–10 minutes. Cool on a wire tray and then dip the cookies in melted chocolate.

Makes 30.

One Stage Treacle Crisps
6 oz. plain flour
$\frac{1}{2}$ level teaspoon cream of tartar
$\frac{1}{2}$ level teaspoon bicarbonate of soda
$\frac{1}{4}$ level teaspoon salt
4 oz. luxury margarine
6 oz. castor sugar
3 tablespoons black treacle
2 oz. raisins, chopped

Sieve the flour, cream of tartar, bicarbonate of soda and salt into a mixing bowl. Place the remaining ingredients in the bowl and beat together with a wooden spoon until well mixed (approximately 2–3 minutes). Gather the mixture together with the fingertips and form into a roll.

To freeze:
Cut the roll into 4 pieces and place dividing papers between them. Wrap the rolls in moisture-vapour-proof paper or aluminium foil. If wrapped in moisture-vapour-proof paper, seal before freezing.

To prepare for cooking:
Unwrap and thaw at room temperature until the dough is soft enough to slice. Cut thinly and place the cookies fairly wide apart on a greased baking sheet. Bake in the centre of a

moderately hot oven (375 deg. F. – Gas Mark 5) for 7–10 minutes. Cool on a wire tray.

Makes 36–40.

Date and Nut Loaf
1 lb. plain flour
1 teaspoon salt
2 level teaspoons baking powder
4 oz. butter *or* margarine
4 oz. soft brown sugar
6 oz. cooking dates, chopped
2 oz. walnuts, chopped
1 egg
scant $\frac{1}{2}$ pint milk

Sieve the flour, salt and baking powder into a mixing bowl. Rub the butter into the flour, add the sugar, dates and walnuts. Make a well in the centre, add the egg and sufficient milk to make a soft dough. Turn the dough on to a floured board and knead lightly, shape into a roll and place in a greased 2-lb. loaf tin. Bake in the centre of a moderately hot oven (375 deg. F. – Gas Mark 5) for 50–60 minutes.

To freeze:
Cool completely and wrap in moisture-vapour-proof paper, double or heavy duty foil or thick polythene. Seal and freeze.

To prepare for serving:
Thaw, still wrapped, at room temperature allowing approximately 6 hours.

Makes a 2-lb. loaf.

Banana Fruit Loaf
8 oz. self-raising flour
$\frac{1}{2}$ teaspoon salt
pinch mixed spice
4 oz. castor sugar
1 heaped tablespoon golden syrup
2 oz. peel, chopped
2 oz. walnuts, coarsely chopped
2 oz. glacé cherries, washed and quartered
4 oz. luxury margarine, sliced
1 lb. bananas, mashed
2 eggs

Sieve the flour, salt and spice into a mixing bowl. Dry the cherries and add to the bowl with the remaining ingredients then beat with a wooden spoon, until evenly mixed. Spread in a 2-lb. greased loaf tin and bake in the centre of a moderate oven (350 deg. F. – Gas Mark 4) for $1\frac{1}{2}$–$1\frac{3}{4}$ hours.

To freeze:
Cool completely. Wrap in moisture-vapour-proof paper, a double thickness of foil, or thick polythene. Seal and freeze.

To prepare for serving:
Thaw, still wrapped, at room temperature allowing approximately 6 hours.

Makes a 2-lb. loaf.

Feather Sponge
5 oz. plain flour
1 oz. cornflour
2 level teaspoons baking powder
$\frac{1}{2}$ level teaspoon salt
5 oz. castor sugar
2 eggs, separated
6 tablespoons corn oil
6 tablespoons water

Line the bottom of two 7-inch sandwich tins with greaseproof paper and grease lightly. Sieve the dry ingredients into a bowl. Mix together lightly with a fork, the egg yolks, corn oil and water.
Stir this mixture into the dry ingredients. Whisk the egg whites until stiff, fold lightly into the mixture. Turn the mixture into the prepared tins. Bake in a moderately hot oven (375 deg. F. – Gas Mark 5) for 25–30 minutes. Remove from tins, allow to cool on a wire tray. Sandwich together with jam.

To freeze:
Wrap in a polythene bag with all the air excluded. Tightly seal and freeze.

To prepare for serving:
Thaw, wrapped, at room temperature for 4–6 hours.

Makes a 7-inch cake.

Gingerbread
4 oz. margarine
6 oz. black treacle
2 oz. golden syrup
$\frac{1}{4}$ pint milk

Gingerbread

2 eggs
8 oz. plain flour
2 oz. brown sugar
1 rounded teaspoon mixed spice
1 level teaspoon bicarbonate of soda
2 level teaspoons ground ginger
4 oz. sultanas (optional)

Grease and line a 7-inch square cake tin. Warm together margarine, treacle and syrup. Add milk and cool. Beat eggs and blend with mixture. Sieve dry ingredients together, add the cooled mixture and blend with a tablespoon. Add fruit if required. Turn into the prepared tin. Bake in the centre of a slow oven (300 deg. F. – Gas Mark 2) for $1\frac{1}{4}$–$1\frac{1}{2}$ hours.

To freeze:
Turn out of the tin and cool on a wire tray. Wrap in a polythene bag with all air excluded. Tightly seal and freeze.

To prepare for serving:
Thaw sealed at room temperature for 4–6 hours. Top with water icing and chopped almonds.

Makes a 7-inch square cake.

43

Scones

1 lb. plain flour
1 level teaspoon salt
2 level teaspoons bicarbonate of soda *and*
    4 level teaspoons cream of tartar *or*
    8 level teaspoons baking powder
3 oz. castor sugar
3 oz. butter or margarine
2 eggs, plus sufficient milk to make ½ pint

Sift flour, salt, bicarbonate of soda and cream of tartar (or baking powder) together. Stir in sugar. Rub in the fat. Beat eggs and milk lightly together. Make a well in the centre of the flour mixture and pour the liquid into it. Stir lightly together to make a dough just firm enough to handle. Turn out on a floured board, roll or pat out by hand to ⅜-inch thickness. Cut into 2- to 2½-inch rounds, bake on a floured baking sheet in a fairly hot oven (400 deg. F. – Gas Mark 6) for 7–10 minutes. Cool on a wire tray.

To freeze:
Pack into polythene bags or other suitable containers. Seal and freeze.

To prepare for serving:
Thaw, covered, at room temperature for about 2 hours.   Makes 16–20.

Plum Cake Ring

6 oz. butter or margarine
6 oz. soft brown sugar
3 large eggs
8 oz. self-raising flour
1 teaspoon baking powder
1 teaspoon mixed spice
8 oz. sultanas
6 oz. currants
4 oz. mixed cut peel
2 oz. glacé cherries
4 oz. walnuts, chopped
1 miniature bottle rum
To decorate:
crystallised fruits
castor sugar

Cream the butter and sugar until light and fluffy. Lightly whisk the eggs and beat into the butter and sugar mixture gradually. Sieve the flour, baking powder and mixed spice; fold into the creamed ingredients. Stir in the remaining ingredients and spoon the mixture into a greased and floured 3-pint ring mould. Or grease and flour the outside of a 1 lb. cocoa tin, weight it, and place centrally in a prepared 9-inch cake tin. Bake in a hot oven (400 deg. F. – Gas Mark 6) for 15 minutes then reduce the temperature to 300 deg. F. – Gas Mark 2 for a further 2½–2¾ hours. Cool slightly before removing from the tin.

To freeze:
Wrap tightly with moisture-vapour-proof paper and seal with freezer tape or wrap in a double thickness of foil. Store in a biscuit tin or other suitable container until frozen hard.

To prepare for serving:
Thaw, wrapped, at room temperature. Pile crystallised fruits in the centre and sift with castor sugar.   Serves 18–20.

Chocolate Cake

8 oz. self-raising flour
2 oz. cocoa powder
6 oz. castor sugar
½ level teaspoon salt
4 oz. luxury margarine
¼ pint plus 5 tablespoons milk
3 eggs
1½ tablespoons treacle

Grease an 8-inch square or round cake tin. Line bottom with greased paper. Sieve dry ingredients into a large mixing bowl. Add remaining ingredients and beat until well combined. Pour into prepared tin. Bake slowly on middle shelf of oven at (300 deg. F. – Gas Mark 2) for approximately 1¼–1½ hours. Cool in tin for 5 minutes then turn out on to wire tray.

To freeze:
Cool and freeze in a polythene bag with all air excluded. Tightly seal and freeze.

To prepare for serving:
Allow to thaw at room temperature for 4–6 hours. Makes an 8-inch square or round cake.

Chapter Five
Hostess menus

Dinner parties these days tend to be more the informal "come in for an evening meal" type than the grand affairs they used to be. Since cooking has become a delightful hobby to so many people, a small dinner for four or six at the most, gives many a dedicated cook the chance to display his or her talents to an appreciative audience. This makes it much more fun to give such a party, than if one looks on it purely as a social obligation.

There was a time when people were brought up to consider it vulgar to talk enthusiastically about food, or even notice that they were eating as a guest in someone else's home. Nowadays people will freely discuss the menu and compliment a hostess on her cooking as well as exchanging gastronomic reminiscences and treasured recipes. In fact, the subject of food will often take precedence over the traditional rather dull dinner party conversation.

My selection of menus and suitable dishes, therefore, avoids the more obvious choices, such as prawn cocktail, which figure in every hostess's repertoire. The quantities are for six people, and most of the dishes are unusual enough to make an agreeable talking point during the meal, and afterwards.

The three-course dinner is now generally accepted as suitable for even formal entertaining at home (your husband's wealthy relatives; his boss; anyone in fact you don't know well and would like to impress). But just because the freezer makes it so easy, I have included one four-course menu, in case you feel like serving a hot savoury, just for a change. Any of the other menus can be extended to four courses by serving a tempting cheese platter (some English and some foreign cheeses, please) or a beautiful bowl of fresh fruit as dessert if the meal has been rather a substantial one.

To impress your guests the fruit bowl should contain one rather unusual or expensive fruit. A pineapple as a centrepiece, for instance, looks extremely attractive, although at times these are quite cheap; Chinese gooseberries or lychees in their mysterious prickly brown overcoats are now sold in most large towns in season, or the gorgeous crimson or orange-skinned plums and nectarines which are now accepted arrivals on the midwinter scene. For the rest, add crisp, juicy, apples, pears, oranges, and ripe but still firm bananas to round out the selection.

Menus for special dinner parties
The following three menus are planned to give perfect balance to each meal. Reap the rewards of your labours and surprise your guests by serving luxury foods out of season.

Menu 1
Chicken Liver Pâté
Individual Quiches
Apricot Dessert

Menu 2
Gazpacho
Chicken with Lemon Cream
French Apple Pie

Menu 3
Silberbissen
Coquilles St. Jacques
Strawberries Romanoff
Délices de Fromage

MENU 1
Chicken Liver Pâté
1 small onion, finely chopped
2 tablespoons corn oil
4–6 oz. fresh chicken livers
1 level dessertspoon flour
1 yolk hard-boiled egg, mashed
6 oz. butter, softened
1 tablespoon sherry
2 tablespoons double cream
salt and pepper to taste
1 clove of garlic, chopped (optional)

Fry the onion in the oil until golden, and remove from the pan. Trim the livers; wash, dry and coat in the flour. Put the livers in the pan, cover and cook gently for 5–6 minutes. When lightly cooked, chop roughly and pass them, with the onions, through a sieve. Add the hard-boiled egg yolk, butter, sherry, cream and seasoning. Mix together thoroughly until completely smooth and well blended or put into an electric blender.

To freeze:
Pack in a foil pudding basin. Seal with double thickness of foil and freeze.

To prepare for serving:
Thaw at room temperature allowing 3–4 hours. Serve with toast.   Serves 6.

Individual Quiches
6 oz. shortcrust pastry
1 tablespoon corn oil
1 small onion, finely chopped
2 rashers of streaky bacon, finely chopped
1 egg yolk
½ pint milk
1 tablespoon parsley, chopped
½ teaspoon salt
pinch pepper
1 oz. cheese, grated

Roll out the pastry and line six 3-inch patty tins. Bake blind with baking beans in a fairly hot oven (400 deg. F. – Gas Mark 6) for 5 minutes. Remove the baking beans and bake for a further 5 minutes. Heat the corn oil. Add the onion and bacon and fry without browning. Remove from the pan and drain.

Whisk the egg yolk and milk. Stir in the onion, bacon, parsley, salt, pepper and cheese. Divide the mixture between the six pastry cases. Bake in a moderately hot oven (375 deg. F. – Gas Mark 5) for 15 minutes, or until the filling is set. Cool on a wire tray.

To freeze:
When cold, freeze in a biscuit tin until solid, then arrange in a plastic or foil container. Return to the freezer.

To prepare for serving:
Thaw covered, at room temperature and, if liked, warm gently before serving. Garnish each quiche with a slice of tomato.   Serves 6.

Apricot Dessert
1 lb. apricots
¼ pint water
3 oz. castor sugar
little milk
1½ oz. cornflour
2 eggs, separated
¼ pint single cream
1 dessertspoon apricot brandy (optional)

Halve and stone the apricots. Place in a saucepan with the water and sugar. Cover and cook slowly for 15 minutes or until tender. Rub the apricots through a sieve. Make up the purée to 1 pint with milk. Blend the cornflour and egg yolks with a little of the apricot purée. Heat the remainder. Stir in the blended cornflour and bring to the boil, stirring. Cook for a further 3 minutes, stirring all the time to prevent lumps from forming. Pour into a large mixing bowl and leave to cool. Stir in the cream and apricot brandy, if used. Whisk the egg whites until stiff and fold lightly into the apricot mixture. Pour into a dampened 1-lb. loaf tin and chill.

To freeze:
Cover closely with a double or heavy duty foil. Freeze.

To prepare for serving:
Thaw, uncovered, at room temperature allowing approximately 6 hours. Turn out of the tin and decorate with fresh fruit and whipped cream.   Serves 6.

MENU 2
Gazpacho
¼ pint olive oil
3 cloves garlic, crushed
1 small onion, very finely chopped
1 level teaspoon salt
5 tablespoons vinegar
1 large ripe avocado pear, peeled and
   de-seeded
1 15-oz. can tomatoes
1 15-oz. can tomato juice

Beat thoroughly with a rotary beater, or liquidise in a blender, the oil, garlic, onion, salt and vinegar. Dice the flesh from the avocado pear. Beat or liquidise the canned tomatoes, tomato juice and avocado pear. Press through a sieve. Blend the two mixtures together in two batches, if necessary.

To freeze:
Pour into a polythene bag, plastic container or waxed carton. Seal leaving 1-inch headspace and freeze.

To prepare for serving:
Thaw overnight in the refrigerator or at room temperature until liquid but still chilled. Stir well and adjust seasoning. Serve sprinkled with fresh chopped parsley and chives.　　Serves 6.

Chicken with Lemon Cream
1½ oz. butter
6 chicken breasts
2 tablespoons dry sherry
3 tablespoons dry white wine
grated zest of 1 lemon
1½ tablespoons lemon juice
salt and pepper to taste
¼ pint single cream
¼ pint double cream

Melt the butter in a frying pan, add the chicken pieces and fry in it until browned all over (approximately 5 minutes). Transfer chicken to a shallow baking tin. Add the sherry, white wine, grated lemon zest and juice and seasoning to taste, to the juices in the pan. Stir well over gentle heat until thoroughly blended. Remove from heat, add cream, stir again and pour over chicken.

To freeze
Cool rapidly, cover and seal the dish with double thickness of foil before freezing.

To prepare for serving:
Thaw at room temperature and transfer to ovenproof serving dish. Sprinkle with 2 oz. grated Gruyère cheese, put in moderate oven (350 deg. F. – Gas Mark 4) for 35 minutes. Brown under the grill. Place a lemon butterfly on each portion, serve with fluffy long grain rice and sprinkle with chopped parsley.

Serves 6.

French Apple Tart

French Apple Tart
1 oz. butter
1 teaspoon cinnamon
4 oz. soft brown sugar
4 large cooking apples
For pastry crust:
5 oz. plain flour
½ teaspoon salt
4 oz. butter
1 egg, lightly beaten
2 tablespoons cold water

Butter a 9-inch sandwich tin and line bottom with a circle of buttered greaseproof paper. Sprinkle with cinnamon and brown sugar. Peel, core and slice the apples as thinly as possible. Cover bottom of the dish with concentric circles of apple slices, pressing them down firmly. Fill tin with more layers of apple slices, well pressed down. Top with rest of the butter.

Make the pastry crust mixing ingredients with a fork as the dough will be very soft. Chill before rolling out to make it easier to handle. Roll out to a circle large enough to fit the dish and press lightly on top.

To freeze:
Wrap in double thickness of foil or sheet polythene. Seal and freeze.

To prepare for serving:
Put pie in a very hot oven (450 deg. F. – Gas Mark 8) while still frozen. Immediately reduce heat to 375 deg. F. – Gas Mark 5. Bake 30–35 minutes, remove from oven and immediately invert on serving dish and remove greaseproof paper. Serve warm if liked with sweetened whipped cream.　　　　　　Serves 6.

Illustrated in colour on the back cover.

MENU 3
Silberbissen
1 large grapefruit, halved
12 oz. cream cheese
3 tablespoons soured cream
1 tablespoon onion, finely chopped
salt and pepper to taste
1 tablespoon lemon juice
2 tablespoons walnut halves, chopped

Remove the grapefruit segments. Beat together cream cheese, soured cream, onion, salt and pepper and lemon juice. Stir in lightly the grapefruit segments and chopped walnuts.

To freeze:
Spoon into waxed cartons. Seal leaving $\frac{1}{2}$-inch headspace and freeze.

To prepare for serving:
Thaw at room temperature and spoon into cocktail glasses lined with shredded lettuce. Serve with fingers of toast.　　　　Serves 6.

48

Butter a 9-inch sandwich tin and line with greaseproof paper.

Sprinkle the base with cinnamon and brown sugar. Cover the bottom of the dish with concentric circles of apple.

Fill the tin with more layers of apple slices, well pressed down. Lightly press the circle of pastry on the top.

Cool and wrap in double or heavy duty foil and overwrap with polythene.

Coquilles St. Jacques

¼ pint dry white vermouth *or*
⅛ pint plus 4 tablespoons of dry white wine
salt and pepper to taste
1 bay leaf
2 tablespoons onion, finely chopped
1 lb. scallops
8 oz. mushrooms, sliced
1½ oz. butter
1½ oz. flour
¼ pint milk
2 egg yolks
¼ pint double cream
1 teaspoon lemon juice

Simmer together for 5 minutes the vermouth or wine, salt, pepper, bay leaf and onion. Add scallops and sliced mushrooms. Add sufficient water just to cover, simmer covered for 5 minutes. Remove scallops and mushrooms and boil stock quickly to reduce to ½ pint. Melt butter, stir in flour, blend in the stock and milk. Cook, stirring, for 1 minute. Remove from heat. Blend egg yolks with cream, gradually stir hot sauce into the egg and cream mixture. Return to pan and reheat for 2 minutes but do not boil, stirring all the time. Season to taste with salt, pepper and lemon juice. Cut scallops into bite-size pieces, stir with mushrooms into the sauce. Butter 6 deep scallop shells, fill with the mixture.

To freeze:
Cool rapidly. Cover closely with double or heavy duty foil and freeze.

To prepare for serving:
Thaw in the refrigerator for about 4 hours, sprinkle with a little grated Gruyère cheese, dot with butter and grill for 15 minutes or until well browned. Serves 6.

Strawberries Romanoff

1½ lb. frozen strawberries (sweetened)
¼ pint orange juice
7 tablespoons Curaçao *or* Cointreau
½ pint double cream
1 oz. icing sugar, sifted

Partially thaw the strawberries. Combine orange juice and liqueur. Pour over the strawberries. Keep chilled. Place in a glass serving dish. Whip the cream and icing sugar and pile on top. Serves 6.

Délices de Fromage

4 slices streaky bacon, trimmed
3 oz. Gruyère cheese, grated
1 oz. Parmesan cheese, grated
1 small onion, grated
1 teaspoon mayonnaise
½ teaspoon dry mustard
6 large slices white bread

Grill bacon until crisp and crush finely. Mix grated cheese, onion and bacon with the mayonnaise and mustard. Toast bread on one side. Trim, halve, spread mixture on untoasted side.

To freeze:
Stack on double thickness of foil, dividing each slice with foil. Wrap, seal and freeze.

To prepare for serving:
Thaw, wrapped, at room temperature. Unwrap, grill, cheese side up, until golden. Serves 6.

Consommé

8–12 oz. shin of beef
2 carrots, sliced
1 leek, sliced
1 stick celery, sliced
2 pints brown stock
4 stalks parsley
1 sprig thyme
½ bay leaf
3–4 egg whites, lightly whisked

Trim the fat from the meat and cut into fine strips. Put it into a saucepan with the vegetables and stock. Tie the parsley stalks, thyme and bay leaf with thread and add to the ingredients in the pan, together with the egg whites. Bring slowly to simmering point, stirring all the time. When the liquid begins to cloud, stop stirring and continue to simmer gently for 10–15 minutes, or until the egg has hardened and the consommé is clear and brilliant. Put a clean, wet cloth over a large mixing bowl and ladle the consommé through it. Do not press the soup through the cloth. Discard the meat and vegetables.

To freeze:

Pack in plastic or waxed cartons. Seal and freeze.

To prepare for serving:

Immerse the container in hot water. Gently reheat contents in a saucepan. Add 3 tablespoons of dry sherry and correct the seasoning before serving. Serves 6.

French Onion Soup

1 oz. margarine
1 lb. onions, skinned and sliced
1½ pints stock *or*
  2 stock cubes plus water
salt to taste
1 oz. cornflour
¼ pint cold water

Melt the margarine in a pan. Add the sliced onions, cover and cook gently for 20–30 minutes until soft but not coloured. Remove lid and allow to cook until brown. Stir in the stock and salt, re-cover and simmer for 30 minutes. Blend the cornflour and water together, stir into the soup. Continue to cook, stirring until thick.

To freeze:

Cool and pour into waxed cartons, plastic or other suitable containers. Seal and freeze.

To prepare for serving:

Gently reheat in a pan. Ladle into soup plates. Serve with slices of toasted French bread and grated Parmesan cheese. Serves 6.

Cream of Cucumber Soup

2 young cucumbers
1 oz. butter
salt and pepper to taste
pinch sugar
¼ pint chicken stock
¼ pint white sauce
green colouring

Wipe and peel the cucumbers, slice in half lengthways, remove seeds. Cut into thick slices, blanch in boiling water for 30 seconds and drain. Melt the butter in a heavy saucepan, add the cucumbers, seasoning and sugar. Cover and cook gently until soft. Add the chicken stock and white sauce. Bring to boil. Pass through a fine sieve, or liquidise in a blender, and return to the saucepan. Thin down with a little more stock if necessary. Check the seasoning and add a little green colouring.

To freeze:

Cool and pack into a waxed or plastic container, leaving 1-inch headspace.

To prepare for serving:

Immerse the container in hot water to loosen the contents. Reheat gently in a saucepan. Add a 2½ oz. carton of single cream and reheat without boiling. Serves 6.

Vichyssoise

6 large leeks
4 medium potatoes
2 oz. butter
1½ pints chicken stock *or*
  2 stock cubes plus water
salt and pepper to taste
To garnish:
1 heaped tablespoon chives, chopped

Trim all green parts from the leeks, wash thoroughly and cut into short lengths. Peel and slice the potatoes. Heat the butter in a saucepan and sauté the leeks gently until soft but not coloured, add the potatoes, chicken stock and seasoning and simmer until the vegetables are tender. Press through a fine sieve or liquidise in an electric blender.

To freeze:

Pack in plastic or waxed containers, leaving 1-inch headspace. Cover and freeze.

To prepare for serving:

Thaw at room temperature, stir in ¼ pint fresh or soured cream. Sprinkle each serving with chopped chives. Serves 6.

Terrine of Pork

Brandied Chicken Liver Pâté

3 oz. streaky bacon, trimmed
1 tablespoon corn oil
1 small onion, finely chopped
1 lb. chicken livers, chopped
2 oz. breadcrumbs
1 egg, lightly beaten
salt and pepper to taste
½ teaspoon powdered mace
1 tablespoon brandy

Stretch the bacon, using a table knife. Line a 1-lb. loaf tin with bacon strips. Heat the corn oil and add the onion. Fry until soft but not brown. Combine with the remaining ingredients. Spoon the mixture into the loaf tin. Cook in a warm oven (325 deg. F. – Gas Mark 3) for 1½ hours. Leave the pâté in the tin, cover with foil and place weights on top. Leave overnight in a refrigerator.

To freeze:

Remove the weights and foil. Turn out of the tin and cut into slices. Wrap in double or heavy duty foil. Seal and freeze.

To prepare for serving:

Thaw, wrapped, at room temperature for about 5–6 hours. Serve with toast. Serves 6–8.

Terrine of Pork

1 lb. lean pork, minced
8 oz. pork sausage meat
4 oz. rolled oats
rind and juice of ½ lemon
salt and pepper to taste
½ teaspoon sage
1 onion, grated
1 egg, beaten
6 oz. streaky bacon rashers

Mix together all the ingredients except the rashers. De-rind and place the rashers on a board, then stretch them by stroking lengthways gently, using a dinner knife. Arrange in a 2 - lb. loaf tin. Carefully press the meat mixture into the tin and level off the top.

Cover with foil and put in a baking tin of water. Cook for 1½ hours in a moderate oven (350 deg. F. – Gas Mark 4). When cooked, place weight on top and leave overnight.

To freeze:

Ease pâté out of loaf tin. Cut into 12 slices. Put moisture-vapour-proof or foil dividers between every slice; wrap closely in double or heavy duty foil. Freeze.

To prepare for serving:

Open the package and spread out the portions. Thaw at room temperature for about 1 hour.

Serves 6.

Glazed Salmon Trout

2½–3 lb. salmon trout, thawed
6 parsley stalks
½ lemon, cut into thick slices
To decorate:
2 level tablespoons powdered gelatine,
  soaked in 2 tablespoons water
2 pints water
juice of ½ lemon
stuffed olives, sliced
1 canned red pimento, sliced
slices of lemon

Wrap the fish in a well sealed foil parcel with the parsley stalks and lemon. Place on a baking sheet and cook in the centre of a moderate oven (350 deg. F. – Gas Mark 4) allowing 20 minutes per lb. Unwrap and cool on a wire tray.

To decorate, heat a little of the water and pour on to the soaked gelatine, stir to dissolve before adding to the rest of the water, with the lemon juice. Leave in a cool place until on the point of setting. Put a clean tray under the wire rack and spoon the jelly over the fish. Decorate with the olives and pimento. Pour the remaining jelly into an oblong tin and allow to set. Turn out of the tin, dice and arrange on the base of the serving dish. Transfer the fish to the serving dish and garnish with lemon slices.   Serves 6–8.

Rice with Mushrooms and Scampi (below)

Tuna and Mushroom Pie (opposite)

Tuna and Mushroom Pie

8 oz. mushrooms, halved
¼ pint milk
1 oz. butter
1 oz. flour
1 2½-oz. carton single cream
grated rind 1 lemon
salt and pepper
2 7-oz. cans tuna steak
8 oz. packet puff pastry

Simmer the mushrooms in the milk until tender, strain and put the mushrooms aside. Melt the butter in a saucepan and stir in the flour. Stir the cream into the milk and gradually pour into the saucepan, stirring continuously. Bring slowly to the boil, reduce the heat and simmer for 2 minutes, stirring constantly. Add the lemon rind and mushrooms, season to taste with salt and pepper, cover and set aside. Break the tuna into large pieces and mix with the mushrooms in a pie dish. Cover with the sauce, Roll out the pastry and cover the pie dish, trim off the excess pastry, knock up the edge with a knife. Decorate with large flutes and pastry leaves.

To freeze:

Chill in the refrigerator until the pastry is firm. Cover closely with sheet polythene and seal before freezing.

To prepare for serving:

Brush the pastry with beaten egg and bake, unthawed, in a very hot oven (450 deg. F. – Gas Mark 8) for 30–40 minutes.   Serves 6

Glazed Salmon Trout

Rice with Mushrooms and Scampi

8 oz. button mushrooms
10 oz. long grain rice
8 oz. butter
12 oz. frozen scampi, thawed
1 tablespoon brandy
1 level tablespoon tomato purée
2 level tablespoons flour
½ pint milk
2 tablespoons oil
salt and pepper
3 tablespoons grated Parmesan cheese

Wash and dry the mushrooms. Cook the rice in boiling salted water until tender (from 14–20 minutes depending on type used). In a saucepan heat 1 oz. of the butter, add the scampi and cook for 2 minutes. Add the brandy and when evaporated stir in the tomato purée and flour. Add the milk, stir and cook for another minute. Cover and simmer gently for 10 minutes. Meanwhile, in another pan, heat 1 oz. butter with 1 tablespoon oil and sauté the mushrooms gently for 3½ minutes; season with salt and pepper. When rice is cooked, drain thoroughly and return to the saucepan with the remaining butter and the cheese. Heat gently until the butter and cheese combine with the rice.

To freeze:
Cool and pack the rice separately in a foil pudding basin. Cover with double or heavy duty foil and freeze. Pack the scampi mixture into a carton. Seal and freeze.

To prepare for serving:
Thaw at room temperature allowing approximately 4–5 hours. Put the rice in a sieve or colander and place over a saucepan of boiling water. Cover and heat through. Add a lightly beaten egg yolk and ¼ pint single cream to the scampi mixture. Reheat in a saucepan. Do not allow to boil. Serves 6.

Prawn Curry

3 pints fresh prawns *or*
  1 8-oz. packet frozen prawns
2 tablespoons corn oil
2 medium onions, chopped
3 level tablespoons cornflour
2 chicken stock cubes
3 level teaspoons curry paste
½ teaspoon salt
1½ tablespoons demerara sugar
1 14-oz. can tomatoes
1 bay leaf
1 pint water

Peel the prawns and remove the veins. (If using frozen prawns, de-frost.) Heat the corn oil. Add the onion and fry until soft without browning. Add the cornflour, stock cubes, curry paste, salt, sugar, tomatoes and bay leaf. Stir in the water and bring to the boil, stirring. Cover and simmer for 30 minutes. Add the prawns and simmer for a further 20 minutes.

To freeze:
Cool, put into a suitable container, cover closely and seal before freezing.

To prepare for serving:
Turn carefully into a saucepan and reheat over gentle heat. Serve with plain boiled rice.

Serves 6.

Boeuf Bourguignon

2 lb. best stewing steak
2 level tablespoons flour
salt and pepper
1½ oz. dripping or lard
4 oz. streaky bacon, diced
12 small onions, or shallots
1 clove garlic, crushed
pinch thyme
½ bay leaf
1 15-oz. can cream of mushroom soup
2 oz. mushrooms, sliced
¼ pint Burgundy

Trim and cut meat into neat 1-inch squares, toss in the seasoned flour and fry in hot fat in a flameproof casserole for a few minutes to seal. Remove the meat from the casserole, and keep hot. Fry the bacon, and return the meat to the casserole. Add six onions, the garlic, thyme, bay leaf, mushroom soup, mushrooms and Burgundy. Cook for 1½ hours in a warm oven (325 deg. F. – Gas Mark 3). Add the remaining onions.

To freeze:
Remove the bay leaf and cool rapidly. Pack in plastic or foil containers. Seal and freeze.

To prepare for serving:
Thaw at room temperature allowing approximately 6 hours for thawing. Cook for 40 minutes in a warm oven (325 deg. F. – Gas Mark 3). Serves 6.

Boeuf Bourguignon

Boeuf Provençal

2 lb. chuck or buttock steak
4 oz. belly of pork
1 tablespoon olive oil
1 11-oz. can tomatoes
¼ pint stock or water
6 parsley stalks *and*
  ½ bay leaf, tied with thread
  to make a bouquet garni
½ teaspoon salt
pinch pepper
½ teaspoon rosemary
¼ pint dry white wine
6 green olives, stoned

Trim and cut the beef into 1-inch cubes. Trim and dice the pork finely. Heat the oil in a large saucepan and add the pork; fry until the fat is rendered down. Add the beef to the pork and fry briskly to brown on all sides. Add the tomatoes, with the juice, the stock, bouquet garni, salt, pepper and rosemary. Cover with a lid and simmer very gently for 1 hour. Add the wine and continue to cook for a further 15 minutes.

To freeze:
Add the olives and cool. Put into a plastic, foil or other suitable container, cover closely and seal before freezing.

To prepare for serving:
Turn into a saucepan, adjust seasoning and thicken with 1 oz. *beurre manié*.* Serves 6.

*To make *beurre manié* work butter and flour together, using 1½ parts of butter to 1 part flour. This can be made in bulk and stored in the refrigerator for up to 6 weeks or it can be stored in the freezer for up to 3 months. Weigh the required amount and stir into soups or stews to thicken.

54

Boeuf Stroganoff (1)

Rich Beef Casserole

2 lb. chuck or buttock steak
1 oz. flour, seasoned
2 tablespoons cooking oil
1 large onion, finely chopped
1 clove garlic
1 teaspoon salt
1 tablespoon tomato purée
1 teaspoon sugar
$\frac{1}{2}$ teaspoon dried basil
pinch pepper
$\frac{1}{2}$ pint stock or water
$\frac{1}{4}$ pint dry red wine

Cut the meat into 1-inch cubes and toss in the seasoned flour. Heat the oil in a large saucepan and when it is very hot, fry the meat to brown on all sides. Lower the heat and add the onion. Crush the garlic with the salt and add it to the ingredients in the pan. Continue to cook until the onion softens. Mix in the tomato purée and add the sugar, basil, pepper and stock. Cover with a lid and simmer over a gentle heat for 45 minutes before adding the wine; cook for a further 30 minutes. Serves 6.

To freeze:

Cool rapidly, put into a suitable plastic container, cover closely and seal before freezing.

To prepare for serving:

Turn into a saucepan and reheat gently.

Boeuf Stroganoff (1)

3 tablespoons cooking oil *or*
    2 oz. butter
1 onion, peeled and sliced
1 small clove garlic, crushed
$1\frac{1}{4}$ lb. stewing steak, cut into thin strips
    $1\frac{1}{2}$ inches long
4 oz. mushrooms, sliced
pinch paprika
2 teaspoons Worcestershire sauce
1 packet tomato soup
$\frac{3}{4}$ pint water

Melt the oil or butter in a saucepan and add the onion, garlic and meat. Cover, and simmer gently for 30 minutes. Add the mushrooms, paprika, Worcestershire sauce and contents of the packet of tomato soup. Gradually stir in water, bring to boil, cover and simmer for 30 minutes or until the meat is tender.

To freeze:

Cool and spoon into a foil, plastic or waxed carton. Seal and freeze.

To prepare for serving:

Heat in a warm oven (325 deg. F. – Gas Mark 3), and add $\frac{1}{4}$ pint yoghourt or soured cream when beef is hot but not bubbling. Serves 6.

Boeuf Stroganoff (2)

1½ lb. rump steak
1 oz. butter *or*
   2 tablespoons salad oil
1 packet Stroganoff sauce mix

Cut the steak into thin strips about ¼ inch by ½ inch thick and 1½ inches long. Brown the meat, using the butter or oil in a frying pan. Put the meat into a flameproof dish. Stir Stroganoff mix into a scant ¾ pint water and add to meat. Bring to boil; reduce heat. Cover and simmer until meat is tender. Remove the meat. Measure the juices and add sufficient water to make up to ½ pint. Return the meat to the dish. Bring to the boil; reduce the heat. Cover and simmer for 10 minutes.

To freeze:

Cool rapidly, cover with the lid and freeze.

To prepare for serving:

If using a pyrosil dish remove the lid before heating. When the meat is hot add ¼ pint soured cream and reheat without boiling.

Serves 6.

Note: This recipe is the anglicised version of the recipe on the sauce mix packet.

Heat oil in a pan and drop in the strips of steak, one at a time. Brown the meat, turning frequently to seal.

Cut steak across in half. Cut thin strips across the grain of the rump from both pieces, until you have as many neat strips as possible.

Mix one packet of Stroganoff Sauce with scant ¾ pint water. Stir well. Pour over the meat. Cover and simmer. Cool quickly.

When the meat is evenly browned turn into a flameproof casserole, with its juices.

When quite cold put into the freezer. To reheat place casserole over gentle heat until just boiling, stir in cream. Bring to boil, serve.

Sauté de Veau Marengo

2 lb. shoulder of veal
2 oz. butter
2 tablespoons oil
2 medium-sized onions, peeled and chopped
1 tablespoon flour
¼ pint dry white wine
1 tablespoon tomato purée
½ bay leaf, *tied together with*
　4 parsley stalks *and*
　1 sprig of thyme
¼ teaspoon basil
salt and pepper
½ teaspoon sugar
8 oz. button mushrooms, washed and trimmed

Cut the meat into 2-inch cubes. Heat the butter and oil together in a large heavy frying pan; add the meat to the pan and brown over a brisk heat. Remove the meat and sauté the onions until soft but not coloured. Sprinkle the flour over the onions and cook gently for 1 minute. Transfer the onion to a saucepan and add the meat to it. Pour the wine over the meat; add tomato purée, bouquet garni, basil, salt, pepper and sugar. Cover the saucepan with greaseproof paper and a tight-fitting lid. Simmer for 1 hour. Halve the mushrooms and add to the saucepan. Continue to cook for 3 minutes.

To freeze:
Cool rapidly and spoon into plastic or other suitable containers, leaving ½-inch headspace. Seal and freeze.

To prepare for serving:
Thaw at room temperature for about 6 hours. Reheat in a saucepan. Garnish with triangles of fried bread before serving.　　Serves 6.

Stuffed Fillet of Pork

1 lb. pork tenderloin
2 oz. butter or margarine
1 medium onion, peeled and finely chopped
4 oz. mushrooms, thinly sliced
1 oz. flour
½ pint chicken stock
pinch pepper
½ teaspoon salt

For the filling:

1 small onion, peeled and finely chopped
8 oz. streaky bacon, cooked and diced
3 tablespoons breadcrumbs
4 oz. sausage meat
¼ teaspoon salt
¼ teaspoon mixed herbs
1 egg, beaten

Trim and cut the pork into 6 pieces. Beat each piece between two sheets of wet grease-proof paper until very thin.

Combine all the ingredients for the filling and spread equal portions on to each piece of pork. Fold opposite sides to overlap, then tuck the ends over, parcel-fashion. Secure with cocktail sticks.

Melt the butter in a saucepan and cook the pork briskly until brown on all sides. Remove from the pan. Add the onion and mushrooms to the pan and cook gently until soft, but not coloured. Return the pork to the pan, add the flour, liquid and seasoning. Cover with a tight-fitting lid and simmer for 15 minutes.

To freeze:
Cool rapidly. Pack into plastic or other suitable containers, leaving ½-inch headspace. Seal and freeze.

To prepare for serving:
Immerse the container in hot water. Gently reheat in a saucepan. Serve with plain boiled rice. Serves 6.

Sautéed Sweetbreads

1½ lb. sweetbreads
¾ pint chicken stock *or*
   1 stock cube plus water
1½ oz. flour, seasoned
beaten egg and breadcrumbs for coating

Soak the sweetbreads in salted, cold water for 1 hour. Drain and rinse. Put the sweetbreads in a saucepan, cover with water and bring to the boil. Drain and cool. Remove any fat. Simmer in the stock for 25 minutes or until tender. Drain, cool and cut into bite-size pieces. Toss in seasoned flour, dip in egg and coat with breadcrumbs.

To freeze:
Pack in a polythene bag. Seal tightly and freeze.

To prepare for serving:
Thaw, covered, in the refrigerator, overnight. Fry in butter and serve with tomato sauce. Serves 6.

Chicken Paprika

1 3-lb. chicken
cornflour for coating
salt and pepper
2 tablespoons corn oil
1 onion, sliced
1 chicken stock cube
1 10-oz. can tomatoes, drained
1 green pepper, sliced
¼ level teaspoon garlic salt
1 level tablespoon paprika pepper
½ pint water

Joint the chicken and coat with the cornflour to which salt and pepper have been added. Heat the corn oil in a large saucepan and brown the chicken pieces on both sides. Remove from the pan.

Add the onion to the pan and cook until tender. Add the chicken stock cube, tomatoes, pepper, garlic salt and paprika pepper. Stir in the water.

Return the chicken to the pan, cover and simmer gently for 40–50 minutes or until the chicken is tender. Remove chicken joints and boil the sauce in the pan rapidly until it is reduced by half.

To freeze:
Cool rapidly, put into a suitable container, cover closely and seal before freezing.

To prepare for serving:

Turn into a saucepan and reheat gently. Plain boil 12 oz. Patna rice and put it around the edge of the serving dish. Place the chicken joints in the centre. Add $\frac{1}{4}$ pint soured cream to sauce and reheat without boiling. Pour over the chicken. Serves 6.

Chicken with Pineapple

2 oz. butter or margarine
1 small green pepper, de-seeded and sliced
2 oz. flour
$\frac{1}{2}$ pint milk
$\frac{1}{2}$ pint chicken stock
1$\frac{1}{2}$ lb. cooked chicken, diced
12 oz. can pineapple cubes, drained
salt and pepper to taste

Heat the butter and fry the sliced pepper gently for 5 minutes. Set aside and stir the flour into the butter. Combine the milk and chicken stock and gradually add to the flour and butter. Stir over a moderate heat until the sauce is smooth and thick. Add the green pepper, chicken, pineapple, salt and pepper and a little of the fruit juice if liked.

To freeze:

Cool quickly. Pack into polythene or other suitable containers, leaving $\frac{1}{2}$-inch headspace.

To prepare for serving:

Turn into double boiler and heat through, for approximately 30 minutes. Serves 6.

Poulet Sauté Grand Monarque

1 oz. butter
1 tablespoon cooking oil
6 chicken pieces
1 medium onion, peeled and finely chopped
6 button onions, peeled
6 button mushrooms, washed and trimmed
3 tablespoons brandy
$\frac{1}{4}$ teaspoon tarragon
$\frac{1}{4}$ pint stock or water
$\frac{1}{2}$ teaspoon salt
$\frac{1}{4}$ pint dry, white wine

Heat the butter and oil in a large frying pan. When very hot add the chicken pieces and fry to brown on all sides. Transfer the chicken to an ovenproof dish. Lower the heat and sauté the chopped onion until soft but not brown; add the button onions and cook until golden. Spoon the onions into the dish with the chicken. Fry the mushrooms gently for 2 minutes; set aside.

Pour the brandy over the chicken and set alight. When the flames have died down add the remaining ingredients, with the exception of the wine. Cover with a lid and cook in the centre of a moderate oven (350 deg. F. – Gas Mark 4) for 45 minutes. Add the wine and continue to cook for a further 15 minutes.

To freeze:

Add mushrooms and cool rapidly. Put into a suitable container, cover closely and seal before freezing.

To prepare for serving:

Turn into a saucepan and reheat gently. Correct the seasoning and thicken with 1 oz. *beurre manié* (see page 00). Lower the heat and simmer for 10–12 minutes. Serves 6.

Chicken Chop Suey

1 large head celery, cut into thin strips
3 large onions
salt and pepper to taste
1 level tablespoon sugar
2 pints chicken stock *or*
   2 stock cubes plus water
1 can bean sprouts
1 can bamboo shoots
1 lb. cooked chicken, cut into fine strips
1$\frac{1}{2}$ oz. cornflour
3 tablespoons cold water
2 tablespoons soy sauce

Clean and cut celery into thin strips. Peel and finely slice onions. Simmer celery, onion, salt, pepper and sugar in the stock and the liquid from the cans of bean sprouts and bamboo shoots for 20 minutes. Add the chicken, bean sprouts and finely chopped bamboo shoots to the vegetable mixture. Blend the cornflour with the cold water and stir into the mixture. Simmer gently for 10 minutes, stirring frequently. Add the soy sauce.

To freeze:
Cool rapidly, pack in a large plastic container. Seal and freeze.

To prepare for serving:
Thaw at room temperature allowing approximately 6 hours. Reheat gently in a covered saucepan. Serves 6.

Jugged Hare
1 hare, skinned and jointed (reserve blood)
salt and pepper to taste
bouquet garni
2 stock cubes (optional)
seasoned flour
8 oz. streaky bacon, diced
3 carrots, peeled and sliced
1 large onion, stuck with 6 cloves
sprig of thyme
pinch mace
$\frac{1}{4}$ pint red wine
4 oz. redcurrant jelly

Use the carcass and head of the hare to make stock, seasoning well with salt, pepper and a bouquet garni, or use two beef stock cubes to $1\frac{1}{4}$ pints boiling water.

Turn the joints in seasoned flour. Fry bacon gently, set aside, retaining dripping. Fry joints of hare in the rendered fat in a saucepan or flameproof casserole to seal all surfaces. Add to the bacon with the carrots, onion, herbs and seasoning.

Pour in enough stock just to cover, put on lid, and simmer gently for $2-2\frac{1}{2}$ hours according to the size and age of the hare. Ten minutes before it is ready, mix together the blood, red wine and redcurrant jelly and add to the hare, to thicken the sauce.

To freeze:
Remove the joints and reduce the sauce slightly, if desired, by further simmering. Cool rapidly, either freeze in the casserole or put into some other suitable container. Cover closely and seal before freezing.

To prepare for serving:
Turn into a saucepan, reheat carefully over gentle heat. Serves 6.

Casserole of Pigeons
4 oz. pork
4 oz. veal
3 wood pigeons, cleaned
4 oz. streaky bacon, stretched
1 oz. seasoned flour
2 oz. butter
$\frac{1}{2}$ pint chicken stock (see page 27)
1 onion
1 carrot
6 parsley stalks
salt and pepper to taste
8 oz. mushrooms

Finely mince the pork and the veal together. Divide the mixture into three and put a portion in the body cavity of each bird. Cover the breasts with bacon and secure with string. Coat the birds with seasoned flour, melt 1 oz. of the butter in the casserole and brown the birds, on all sides, over a brisk heat. Add the stock, onion, carrot, parsley stalks and seasoning. Cover with a lid and bake in the centre of a moderate oven (325 deg. F. – Gas Mark 3) for $2-2\frac{1}{2}$ hours.

Remove the pigeons from the casserole dish; remove the bacon, cut into dice and set aside. Cut the pigeons in half, down the centre. Melt the remaining butter in a small saucepan, add the mushrooms and cook for $1\frac{1}{2}$ minutes.

To freeze:
Put the pigeons into a small baking tin with the bacon, mushrooms and strained liquor. Cool rapidly. Cover and seal with foil before freezing.

To prepare for serving:
Partially thaw at room temperature allowing approximately 2 hours. Reheat in a moderate oven (350 deg. F. – Gas Mark 4). Serves 6.

Baked Alaska
1 8-inch sponge cake
1 tablespoon raspberry jam
1 family brick ice cream

Spread the base of the cake with the jam. Mash the ice cream with a fork and spread on top of the jam.

To freeze:
Place on a baking sheet and freeze until firm, then wrap with foil.

To prepare for serving:
Whisk two egg whites stiffly and gradually add 3 oz. castor sugar whilst still whisking. When the meringue is stiff and shiny, remove the base from the freezer, unwrap and spoon the meringue on top. Cook in the top of a preheated very hot oven (450 deg. F. – Gas Mark 8) for 3–5 minutes or until brown. Serve immediately. Serves 6.

Rum Sponge
3 eggs
6 oz. castor sugar
3 oz. plain flour
¼ pint water
2 tablespoons rum

Put the eggs and half the sugar in a mixing bowl over a saucepan of hot water. Whisk until the mixture is thick enough to leave a trail. Sieve the flour on to the surface of the mixture and carefully fold it in.
Pour into a greased 8-inch savarin tin and bake in the centre of a moderately hot oven (375 deg. F. – Gas Mark 5) for 30–35 minutes or until firm to the touch and golden brown in colour. Remove from the tin and cool on a wire tray.
Dissolve the remaining sugar in the water. Bring to the boil and continue to boil rapidly for 7 minutes, add the rum. Cool, and then prick holes in the sponge with a skewer. Brush with the rum-flavoured syrup until it is all absorbed into the cake.

To freeze:
Wrap tightly in double or heavy duty foil, moisture-vapour-proof paper or thick polythene. Seal and freeze.

To prepare for serving:
Thaw, covered, at room temperature allowing approximately 8 hours. Unwrap and place on a serving dish. Top with peeled and quartered pears frozen in syrup. Use for decoration orange segments and glacé cherries.
Serves 6–8.

Frozen Mocha Sponge Pudding
1 4-oz. packet chocolate chips
4 tablespoons strong coffee
2 sponge cakes, baked in 7×11-inch
   Swiss roll tins
8 oz. unsalted butter
1 lb. icing sugar, sieved
2 egg yolks

Soften the chocolate in a basin, over a saucepan of hot water. When melted, gradually add the coffee. Trim the edges of both sponges and cut them across the width. Cream the butter until soft, then gradually work in the icing sugar and egg yolks. Beat the chocolate into the mixture.
Spread one piece of sponge with one-third of the chocolate filling, then build up the layers pressing each piece of sponge firmly in place on top of the filling. Finish with a sponge layer.

To freeze:
Fit into a rectangular cake tin or carton until frozen, then wrap in double or heavy duty foil and replace in the freezer.

To prepare for serving:
Thaw wrapped at room temperature, for 4–5 hours. Sieve icing sugar over the top. Serves 6.

Lemon Chiffon Pie
1 lemon
2 eggs, separated
2 oz. castor sugar
2 level teaspoons gelatine *dissolved in*
   2 tablespoons hot water
1 baked 9-inch flan case

Squeeze the lemon juice into a mixing bowl and add half the zest, finely grated. Add the egg yolks and sugar and beat, over a saucepan of hot water, until light and fluffy. Remove from the heat and continue to whisk until cool. Whisk the egg whites stiffly. Whisk the gelatine into the egg yolk mixture and continue to whisk until it is on setting point. Quickly fold in the egg whites; turn the mixture into the flan case and chill until set. Partly freeze.

To freeze:
Cover the filling with freezer cellophane and wrap the pie in double or heavy duty foil to seal before returning to the freezer.

To prepare for serving:
Thaw in wrapping, at room temperature for 4 hours. Decorate with whipped double cream.

Serves 6.

Lemon Soufflé
4 level tablespoons cornflour
6 eggs, separated
1 lb. 2 oz. castor sugar
1½ pints milk
6 lemons
¾ oz. gelatine, *dissolved in*
 9 tablespoons of hot water

Blend the cornflour, egg yolks and the sugar with a little of the cold milk. Put the remaining milk on to heat with the lemon rind, pared into thin strips. When the milk is almost boiling, strain off the lemon rind and pour milk on to the blended cornflour, while stirring. Return the mixture to the pan, bring to boil, and cook for 3 minutes, stirring all the time. Pour the mixture into a large bowl. Stir in the dissolved gelatine and juice from the lemons. Leave to cool. Whisk the egg whites until stiff. Fold into the cooled mixture.

To freeze:
Pour into a suitable plastic container and leave in a cool place to set. Cover closely and freeze.

To prepare for serving:
Remove the covering and thaw at room temperature allowing approximately 5 hours. Dip the base of the container into warm water and unmould on to a flat plate. Decorate with whipped cream.

Serves 8.

Chocolate Ice Cream
4 oz. margarine
6 oz. castor sugar
6 oz. plain chocolate
4 eggs, separated
½ teaspoon vanilla essence
½ pint evaporated milk, scalded

Cream the margarine and sugar until light and fluffy. Melt the chocolate in a basin, over a

Chocolate Ice Cream

saucepan of hot water. Stir the chocolate into the egg yolks and add the vanilla essence. Whisk the evaporated milk and fold into the chocolate mixture. Pour into a polythene container, cover and freeze for 1 hour. Remove from the freezer and mash with a fork. Whisk the egg whites stiffly and fold into the mixture. Seal and return to the freezer. Serves 6.

Coffee Ice Cream Charlotte
1 tablespoon apricot jam, sieved
19 Boudoir biscuits
Coffee Ice Cream:
4 eggs, separated
4 oz. icing sugar, sieved
4 tablespoons bottled coffee essence
3 tablespoons rum
½ pint double cream, lightly whipped

Brush sides of 6-inch cake tin with warmed apricot jam. Trim biscuits to depth of tin then stand round side of tin so they fit closely. Whisk egg whites until very stiff, then gradually whisk in icing sugar. Whisk egg yolks, coffee essence and rum together, then whisk gradually into egg whites. Fold in cream.

To freeze:
Pour into middle of cake tin and store in the tin with top tightly covered with foil.

To prepare for serving:
Carefully loosen round side of tin with a palette knife, then dip bottom of tin quickly in warm water. Turn out on to serving plate. Decorate top with whipped cream and toasted almonds.   Serves 6–8.

Orange Flummery
3½ level teaspoons gelatine
1 19½-oz. can orange juice
4 oz. castor sugar
2 level tablespoons cornflour
2 eggs, separated

Mix 1½ teaspoons of the gelatine with ¼ pint plus 2 tablespoons of the orange juice in a small saucepan. Add 1 oz. of the sugar and heat to dissolve without boiling. Pour into the base of a 2-pint mould, cool, and put in the refrigerator to set. Heat the remaining gelatine in the same saucepan, with 6 tablespoons of orange juice. Leave to cool. In a mixing bowl, blend the cornflour with a little of the juice. Dissolve the rest of the sugar in the remaining juice, bring to the boil, then pour on to the cornflour. Return to the pan, bring back to the boil and cook for 2 minutes, stirring constantly. When the mixture has cooled slightly, beat in the egg yolks, stir in the gelatine mixture and put in a cool place.

When it begins to thicken, whisk the egg whites stiffly, carefully fold into the mixture. Pour into the mould and leave to set.
To freeze:
Seal the mould with double or heavy duty foil and freeze.
To prepare for serving:
Thaw overnight in the refrigerator. Turn out on to a serving dish.   Serves 6.

Lemon Sorbet
8 oz. granulated sugar
1 pint water
2 lemons
1 egg white

Dissolve the sugar in water over a gentle heat. Pare the rind thinly from one of the lemons and add it to the sugar. Boil rapidly for 10 minutes, to form a light syrup. Strain into a mixing bowl, allow to cool and freeze for 2 hours. Remove the sorbet from the freezer and whisk to break down the ice particles. Whisk the egg white stiffly and fold into the sorbet with the strained juice of both lemons. Spoon the mixture into a 1½-pint container. Cover closely with foil and re-freeze.   Serves 6.

Orange Flummery

Strawberry Cream Torte

5 egg whites
pinch cream of tartar
8 oz. castor sugar
2 oz. flaked almonds, browned

For the filling:

1 level tablespoon gelatine *dissolved in*
    2 tablespoons hot water
½ pint double cream
½ pint single cream
1 tablespoon castor sugar
3 tablespoons Curaçao
1 lb. fresh strawberries, sliced

Grease and flour two baking sheets. Trace two 6-inch circles on each. Pre-heat the oven to 225 deg. F. – Gas Mark ¼.

Whisk the egg whites and cream of tartar until fluffy, add a third of the sugar and continue to whisk until stiff. Add another third of the sugar and whisk until the mixture is shiny and heavy. Fold in the remaining sugar. Spread the mixture evenly within the traced circles and sprinkle with flaked almonds. Cook in the bottom of the oven for 2–3 hours or until crisp. Remove from the baking sheet and cool on a wire tray.

Dissolve the gelatine in the water and leave to set. Whisk the double and single cream until thick enough to leave a trail. Melt the gelatine in a small saucepan, without boiling; mix into cream with the sugar and the Curaçao. Stir until on the point of setting. Sandwich the meringues together, with cream and strawberries between each layer, reserving some cream to coat the sides and top of the torte.

To freeze:

Place on a baking sheet and partially freeze in order to set the cream before over-wrapping with sheet polythene.

To prepare for serving:

Unwrap and serve frozen.   Serves 6–8.

Frozen Christmas Pudding

For One-Stage Chocolate Cake:

2 oz. luxury margarine
2 oz. castor sugar
2 tablespoons rum (optional)

2 oz. self-raising flour *sifted with*
    ½ level teaspoon baking powder
1 heaped tablespoon cocoa *blended with*
    1 tablespoon hot water

For Ice Cream:

2 oz. castor sugar
¾ oz. gelatine *dissolved in*
    4 tablespoons water
1 16-oz. can evaporated milk, chilled
¼ teaspoon almond essence
2 oz. glacé cherries, halved
little red colouring
2 oz. sultanas and currants, mixed
2 teaspoons lemon juice
grated rind 1 lemon

To make the cake, put all ingredients into a bowl and beat with a wooden spoon for about 3 minutes. Put into a greased and lined 7-inch sandwich tin and bake in the centre of a very moderate oven (335 deg. F. – Gas Mark 3) for 25–30 minutes. Remove from the tin and cool. While the cake is cooling, prepare the ice cream. Add sugar and dissolved gelatine to the chilled milk, whisk and put in refrigerator until just beginning to set. Whisk again and divide in half. Add almond essence and cherries to one half, then colour pink. Add remaining ingredients to other half. Pour the pink mixture into a 3-pint pudding basin, cover with cake. Put the other ice cream on top.

To freeze:

Cover the top of the basin with foil and seal.

To prepare for serving:

Put the basin into hot water for about 1 minute, remove foil lid, invert and turn on to a serving plate. Decorate with holly and serve with whipped cream, topped with cinnamon.

       Serves 18–20.

For smaller parties, cook cake mixture in two 5-inch tins for 20 minutes. Divide ice cream mixture between two 1½ pint bowls. Serve one pudding and store the other in the freezer.

Apple and Blackcurrant Mould

½ pint double cream
½ pint frozen apple purée, thawed
1 egg, separated
1 oz. gelatine

¼ pint plus 4 tablespoons water
8 oz. blackcurrants
sugar to taste
1 level dessertspoon cornflour

Whip the cream until thick enough to leave a trail then fold into the apple purée, with the stiffly beaten egg white. Dissolve ½ oz. of the gelatine in 2 tablespoons of water, heat gently to melt and pour into the apple mixture, stir until on the point of setting. Pour into a large mould and place a small mould of the same shape in the centre. Place in the refrigerator and allow to set before removing the smaller mould.

Meanwhile, simmer the blackcurrants in ¼ pint water with sufficient sugar to taste. Blend the cornflour with a little of the juice, add to the blackcurrants, bring to the boil and simmer for 1 minute, stirring constantly. Cool and beat in the egg yolk. Allow the mixture to become completely cold.

Dissolve the remaining gelatine in the rest of the water and heat gently to melt. Add to the blackcurrant mixture and stir until on the point of setting. Pour into the mould and return to the refrigerator to set.

To freeze:
Seal tightly with double or heavy duty foil and freeze.

To prepare for serving:
Thaw overnight in the refrigerator. Cut into slices and serve with boudoir biscuits.
Serves 6–8.

Apple and Chocolate Flan
5 oz. butter
5 oz. castor sugar
2 large eggs, well beaten
4 oz. plain flour
1 oz. cocoa powder
1 teaspoon baking powder
pinch salt
¼ pint milk

Cream together butter and sugar until light and fluffy. Gradually beat in eggs. Sieve together flour, cocoa powder, baking powder and salt and fold into sponge mixture. Stir in milk and turn into a greased 8½-inch flan tin.

Bake in a moderately hot oven (375 deg. F. – Gas Mark 5) for 45 minutes or until sponge is firm to the touch. Cool on a wire tray.

To freeze:
Wrap closely in foil and freeze.

To prepare for serving:
Thaw, covered, at room temperature allowing approximately 3 hours. Poach partially thawed apple slices in syrup until tender (see page 00). Drain and cool. Just before serving, fill the centre of the flan with scoops of ice cream, top with poached apple slices and decorate with grated chocolate.
Serves 6.

Strawberry Soufflé
12 oz. fresh strawberries
castor sugar
1 oz. gelatine *dissolved in*
¼ pint cold water
4 eggs, separated
red colouring
¼ pint double cream, lightly whipped

Tie a greased, double thickness, sheet of greaseproof paper round a 6-inch soufflé dish. Hull and wash the strawberries. Sieve or put into a blender and sweeten the purée to taste. Put the gelatine and water in a basin over a pan of gently simmering water and leave until gelatine has dissolved.

Whisk egg yolks with 3 oz. sugar over a pan of gently simmering water until thick and creamy. Remove from the heat and whisk until cool. Stir in the gelatine and strawberry purée and colour with a little red colouring to give a good pink colour. When the mixture is thick but not set, fold in the whipped cream. Stiffly whisk the egg whites and fold into the mixture. Turn into the prepared soufflé dish. Put in the freezer and partially freeze.

To freeze:
Remove the greaseproof collar, using a knife, dipped in hot water, if necessary. Cover with moisture-vapour-proof paper, seal and replace in the freezer.

To prepare for serving:
Allow to thaw in the refrigerator for 24 hours. Decorate with whipped cream and strawberries.
Serves 6.

Chocolate Cake with Pears and Chocolate Sauce

3 oz. savoy fingers or dry sponge cake
1 oz. plain chocolate
4 oz. castor sugar
2 eggs, separated
2 tablespoons milk
½ oz. gelatine
1 oz. butter
½ teaspoon vanilla essence or 1 teaspoon rum
2 dessert pears, peeled and cored

Use either an ice tray about 7–8 inches long or a 1-lb. loaf tin (the shallow aluminium type). Cut a piece of non-stick lining paper to line the bottom and sides of the tin and give sufficient length to fold over the finished mixture.

Split the savoy fingers or cut the sponge cake into thin slices. Put a layer in the bottom of the prepared tray, with the rounded sides of the savoy fingers next to the paper. Keep the remaining pieces for the top.

Melt the chocolate in a basin over hot water or in a saucepan over a gentle heat. Add 2 oz. sugar, egg yolks and gelatine dissolved in the milk and continue cooking over a gentle heat stirring all the time, until mixture thickens. Cool, stirring occasionally.

Cream together butter and remaining sugar until soft and light. Add to the chocolate mixture, combine thoroughly. Add vanilla essence or rum. Beat the egg whites until stiff and fold them into the mixture. Pour it into the prepared tray and put another layer of fingers or cake on top. Fold over the spare paper to cover the top. Peel pears, halve and remove cores. Poach pears in heavy sugar syrup until tender.

To freeze:
Cover cake with double or heavy duty foil. Seal and freeze. Cool pears quickly, put into a plastic container, leaving ½ inch headspace, and cover with crumpled foil to keep the pears submerged. Cover closely and freeze.

To serve:
Thaw in the refrigerator for 12 hours and turn out cake while still slightly chilled. Top with pears and pour over chocolate sauce (any type of chocolate sauce can be used).   Serves 6.

66

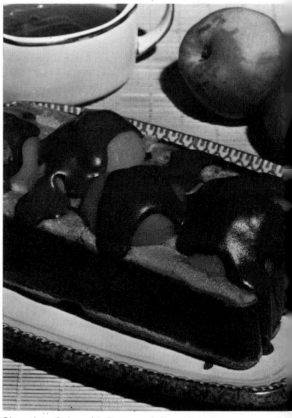

Chocolate Cake with Pears and Chocolate Sauce

Banana Cream

6 bananas
¼ pint double cream, light whipped
¼ pint thick custard (1 tablespoon custard powder to ¼ pint milk)
¼ teaspoon vanilla essence
juice of ½ lemon
2 oz. castor sugar
½ oz. gelatine *dissolved in* ¼ pint hot water

Mash the bananas to a purée with a fork. Blend the banana, whipped cream and cold custard. Add the vanilla essence, lemon juice, and gelatine. Whisk until on the point of setting.

To freeze:
Pour into plastic or foil container. Cover closely and freeze.

To prepare for serving:
Thaw at room temperature for approximately 4 hours.   Serves 6.

Chapter Six
Making more of frozen convenience foods

There seems to be something compulsive about the cooking instructions given on frozen food packs. Most housewives follow the instructions to the letter and would never think of combining the contents of one of these handy packets with other ingredients to produce a more interesting finished dish. Yet there are so many appetising dishes you can prepare using ready-frozen products. For example, your own home-made sweet-and-sour sauce, frozen in small quantities, goes beautifully with crispy cod fries, chicken portions or prawns. Add a big dish of fluffy boiled rice or fried rice and you have a really exotic meal. Even an everyday pleasure like a small tub of mousse can be turned into a party sweet with a crown of piped cream and some fruit.

All the recipes given in this chapter were tested in the experimental kitchens of Birds Eye, the largest supplier of frozen foods in this country. They now run a bulk delivery service of their products to home freezer owners.

Trout Amandine
4 frozen trout, 5–6 oz. each
seasoned flour
3 oz. butter
2 oz. blanched almonds
juice ½ lemon
seasoning
To garnish:
lemon
parsley

Remove the eyes from the frozen trout, coat in seasoned flour. Melt the butter in a pan and fry trout for 7 minutes on either side. Remove from the pan, drain and keep warm on a serving dish. Cut the almonds into shreds, toss in the pan and cook them slowly until a golden brown. Add the lemon juice and seasoning and pour over the fish. Serve garnished with lemon and parsley. Serves 4.

Salmon with Cucumber Sauce
4 frozen salmon steaks, 4–5 oz. each
½ pint water
1 teaspoon lemon juice
little milk
1 oz. butter
1 small onion, finely chopped
½ cucumber, peeled and cut into ¼-inch cubes
1 oz. flour
seasoning
To garnish:
cucumber slices
watercress

Poach the frozen steaks in the water and lemon juice for 12–15 minutes. Remove from the pan, drain, reserving the liquor. Remove skin and bone from the steaks and place on a serving dish, keep warm. Make up fish liquor to ½ pint with a little milk. Melt butter in a saucepan, fry onion until transparent, add cucumber and cook for a further 3 minutes. Stir in the flour, cook for 1 minute. Remove from the heat and blend in the fish liquor and milk. Bring sauce to the boil, stirring, and cook for 3 minutes. Season to taste. Garnish the steaks with cucumber slices and watercress and serve with the sauce. Serves 4.

Kipper Pizzas

For the dough:

½ oz. fresh yeast or 2 teaspoons dried
    yeast and 1 teaspoon sugar
½ pint warm milk
8 oz. plain flour
½ teaspoon salt
½ oz. butter or margarine
1 small egg, beaten

For the filling:

oil
1 11 oz. packet frozen buttered kipper
    fillets, cooked as instructions
1 1¾-lb. can tomatoes, drained
pinch mixed herbs
6 oz. Cheddar cheese, grated
6 gherkins

If using fresh yeast, blend with the warm milk. If using dried yeast, dissolve sugar in milk, sprinkle on dried yeast and leave for 10 minutes until frothy.

Sift flour and salt into a large mixing bowl and rub in the butter or margarine. Mix the yeast liquid and beaten egg together. Make a well in the centre of the flour and pour in the milk and yeast mixture. Mix to a firm dough (until the sides of the bowl are clean). Leave the dough in the bowl in a warm place for 30 minutes, cover with a damp cloth and leave until the dough doubles its size.

Divide the dough into six pieces. Knead each piece and roll out into 5-inch circles. Place on oiled baking sheets and brush with oil. Skin cooked kippers and flake. Cover circles with a layer of tomato mixed with the herbs, then with a layer of flaked kipper and top each with 1 oz. grated cheese. Garnish with slices of gherkin and leave in a warm place for 10 minutes to rise a little. Bake in a moderately hot oven (400 deg. F. – Gas Mark 6) for 18–20 minutes. Serve hot. Makes 6 individual pizzas.

Crispy Cod Fries with Sweet and Sour Sauce

2-inch piece of cucumber, diced
2 medium carrots, cut into strips
½ pint pineapple juice
2 tablespoons white vinegar
5 tablespoons brown sugar
2 teaspoons soy sauce
1 tablespoon cornflour, blended with
    2 tablespoons water
1 7-oz. packet frozen crispy cod fries

Cook the cucumber and carrots in boiling, salted water for 5 minutes, drain.

Place pineapple juice, vinegar and sugar in a pan and heat gently until the sugar has dissolved. Add the soy sauce and blended cornflour and bring to the boil, stirring. Cook for 3 minutes. Add the cucumber and carrot. Cook the crispy cod fries according to the instructions and serve immediately with the sauce. Serves 4.

Cod Steak Crisps

4 large slices lean bacon
1 14-oz. packet frozen cod steaks
1 egg, *beaten with*
    1 tablespoon water
4 oz. potato crisps, finely crushed
oil or fat for frying

Remove rind from the bacon and flatten with the back of a knife. Wrap one rasher around each cod steak. Dip into the egg and water, then coat in the potato crisps. Press well so that the coating remains firm. Shallow fry the fish for 20 minutes, in fat or oil, turning occasionally. Drain and serve immediately. Serves 4.

Cheesy Fish Fingers

1 12-oz. packet frozen fish fingers
2 oz. cheese, grated
1 teaspoon made mustard
1 tablespoon chopped parsley
1 oz. butter, melted
salt and pepper

Grill the fish fingers on one side for 5 minutes. Meanwhile, mix the cheese, mustard, parsley, butter and seasonings in a bowl. Turn the fish fingers and spread some of the mixture on each fish finger. Grill for a further 5 minutes and serve.   Serves 4–6.

Beef Wellington
1 13-oz. packet frozen puff pastry, thawed
For the filling:
2 lb. fillet of beef, cut in one piece
2 oz. butter
4 oz. button mushrooms, sliced
2 teaspoons chopped fresh mixed herbs
beaten egg

Trim fillet and tie up. Melt the butter in a pan and quickly brown the fillet on all sides. Remove from the pan and allow to cool. Fry the mushrooms in the pan for a few minutes and add the herbs; allow to cool.

Roll out the pastry to a rectangle. Mark the pastry lightly into three and cut off one-third. Spread the mushroom mixture on the larger piece, place the beef on top and press the pastry up round it. Damp the edges of the other piece of pastry and place on top. Seal the edges, brush with beaten egg and decorate with 'leaves' made from the pastry trimmings. Bake in a hot oven (425 deg. F. – Gas Mark 7) for 35–40 minutes, or until well browned. Serve immediately.   Serves 6–8.

Chicken Vol-au-Vents
1 13-oz. packet frozen puff pastry, thawed
1 beaten egg
For the filling:
2 frozen chicken quarters, 5 oz. each,
   cooked as instructions
¼ pint cold white sauce
2 tablespoons mayonnaise
seasoning
1 teaspoon chopped parsley
To garnish:
parsley

Roll out the pastry and cut into circles with a 2-inch cutter. Brush half of these with a little water and place on a damp baking sheet. Mark

Mix chicken with white sauce, mayonnaise, seasoning and parsley for filling

Fill generously with chicken mixture and replace the lids

the remaining circles with a 1-inch cutter and place them on top of the circles on the baking sheet. Press gently together. Glaze with beaten egg and bake in a hot oven (425 deg. F. – Gas Mark 7) for 10–12 minutes until risen and golden brown. Remove from baking sheet and allow to cool. Remove the 1-inch 'lids' from the centre of each.

Allow cooked chicken to cool, remove meat from bones and chop. Blend with remaining ingredients and pile into pastry cases. Top with 'lids' and serve. Garnish with parsley.
                                            Makes 20–22.

Coq au Vin

1 oz. butter
1 tablespoon olive oil
6 oz. button onions
4 oz. bacon, cut into strips
4 frozen chicken quarters, 5–6 oz. each,
  thawed
5 tablespoons brandy
1 oz. flour
¾ pint red wine
½ pint stock
1 bay leaf
4 oz. button mushrooms
1 teaspoon sugar
salt and freshly milled black pepper
To garnish:
fried croûtons

Melt the butter in a flameproof casserole, add
the oil and cook the onions with the bacon until
onions are a golden brown. Remove and keep on
a plate. Fry the chicken until lightly browned
on both sides, add the brandy and set alight.
When the flame dies down, remove the chicken
on to the plate, add the flour and cook for
2 minutes. Gradually add the red wine and
stock stirring all the time.

Replace the chicken with the onions and bacon.
Add the mushrooms, bay leaf, sugar and
seasonings. Place the casserole in a warm
oven (325 deg. F. – Gas Mark 3) for 1 hour.
Serve garnished with croûtons round the dish.

Serves 4.

Steaklet Kebabs

1 small green pepper
1 11-oz. packet frozen steaklets
8 rashers streaky bacon, cut in half and
  rolled
8 button mushrooms
8 small onions, parboiled
8 small tomatoes, cut into halves
oil

Remove core and seeds from the pepper and
cut the flesh into pieces approximately 1 inch
square. Cut each steaklet into 4 and arrange
alternately with the other ingredients on 8
small skewers. Brush with oil and grill gently
for 10–15 minutes, turning frequently. Serve
hot. Serves 4 or 8.

70

Put the eggs, onion, sweetcorn, parsley and seasoning
into a basin and mix well

Corn and bacon tarts

Corn and Bacon Tarts

1 7½-oz. packet frozen shortcrust pastry,
  thawed
For the filling:
2 eggs
½ onion, grated
1 6-oz. packet frozen sweetcorn
1 tablespoon chopped parsley
salt and pepper
3 rashers streaky bacon

Roll out the pastry and cut into circles using a
3-inch cutter. Put into patty tins. Put the eggs,
onion, sweetcorn, parsley and seasoning into a
basin. Mix well and spoon into the pastry cases.
Snip the bacon into small pieces and place on
top of the filling. Bake in a moderately hot oven
(375 deg. F. – Gas Mark 5) for 25–30 minutes.
Remove from patty tins and serve hot or cold.

Makes 18.

Souper Sausages

6 oz. spaghetti
1½ oz. butter
1 onion, finely chopped
1 10-oz. packet frozen skinless pork
    sausages, cut in ½-inch pieces
1 10-oz. can condensed tomato soup
few drops Worcestershire sauce
To garnish:
chopped parsley

Cook the spaghetti in boiling, salted water for about 12–15 minutes, drain, toss in ½ oz. of the butter and keep warm on a flat serving dish. Meanwhile, melt the rest of the butter in a pan, add the onion and cook until transparent, but not browned, for about 5 minutes. Add the sausages and cook for a further 5 minutes. Stir in the soup and Worcestershire sauce, heat through and pour the mixture over the spaghetti. Garnish with chopped parsley.

Serves 3–4.

Beefburger Bean Bake

1 16-oz. can baked beans
1 oz. butter or margarine
1 8-oz. packet frozen beefburgers
1 large onion, sliced
4 oz. button mushrooms

Place the baked beans in an ovenproof dish. Melt the butter or margarine, add the beefburgers with the onion and mushrooms and fry gently for 5 minutes turning the beefburgers once. Remove beefburgers and place on the beans.
Cook the vegetables for a further 3 minutes, drain. Place the mushrooms on the beefburgers and onion rings on the mushrooms.
Bake in a moderately hot oven (375 deg. F. – Gas Mark 5) for 15–20 minutes. Serve at once.

Serves 3–4.

Rice Salad

4 oz. Patna rice
1 4-oz. packet frozen diced carrots and peas
1 oz. blanched almonds
3 tablespoons olive oil
1 tablespoon vinegar
1 tablespoon chopped onion
salt and pepper

Cook the rice in boiling, salted water for about 15 minutes until just tender. Drain and cool in running cold water. Cook carrots and peas in boiling, salted water for 7 minutes, drain and cool in running cold water. Cut the almonds into shreds. Mix with the rice and almonds. Blend together the oil and vinegar and stir in the onion and seasoning. Fold dressing into salad and serve.

Serves 4.

Salade Niçoise

1 8-oz. packet frozen sliced green beans
salt
1 15-oz. can new potatoes, drained
1 7-oz. can tuna fish, flaked
1 2-oz. can anchovy fillets, drained and
    soaked in milk
few stoned black olives
4 tablespoons olive oil
2 tablespoons vinegar
pinch pepper
pinch dry mustard
8 oz. small tomatoes, skinned

Cook the beans in boiling, salted water for 5 minutes, drain and cool under running cold water. Cut potatoes into ½-inch cubes, mix with beans and tuna and arrange in a shallow dish. Arrange a lattice of anchovy fillets on top and place the black olives between the lattice. Blend together oil, vinegar and seasonings and spoon over the salad. Cut tomatoes into quarters, remove seeds and arrange around the dish.

Serves 6.

Primavera Salad

1 8-oz. packet frozen broad beans
2 oz. sliced cooked ham
6 tablespoons olive oil
2 tablespoons vinegar
1 teaspoon lemon juice
pinch salt
pinch black pepper
pinch dry mustard
½ teaspoon sugar
1 lettuce
To garnish:
chopped parsley

Cook the beans in boiling, salted water for 7 minutes, drain and cool in running cold water. Cut the ham into strips 1 inch long and mix with the beans. Blend together the oil, vinegar, lemon juice and seasonings and sugar. Pour over the beans and ham and mix together. Wash and dry lettuce and arrange on a plate. Top with bean and ham mixture and sprinkle with chopped parsley to garnish. Serves 4-6.

Prawn Salad
1 lettuce
1 8-oz. packet frozen peeled prawns, thawed
¼ pint mayonnaise
To garnish:
chopped parsley
lemon slices

Wash and dry lettuce. Arrange in a shallow dish and pile the prawns on top, reserving a few for garnish. Coat with mayonnaise, and decorate with chopped parsley, prawns and lemon slices. Serves 6–8.

Tourangelle
¼ pint double cream
¼ pint thick mayonnaise
grated rind and juice ½ lemon
pinch salt
pinch pepper
pinch dry mustard
12 oz. new potatoes
1 8-oz. packet frozen French beans
1 large cooking apple, peeled and sliced
To garnish:
watercress

Stir the cream into the mayonnaise, gradually add the grated rind and juice of the lemon and season well. Scrub the potatoes and boil them in their skins. Cool, peel and cut into ½-inch cubes. Cut the frozen beans into 1-inch pieces and cook for 5 minutes in boiling, salted water. Drain and cool under running cold water. Place potatoes, beans and apple in a serving dish, mix with a little of the lemon mayonnaise and top with the remainder. Garnish with watercress. Serves 5–6.

Cheese Twists
1 13-oz. packet frozen puff pastry, thawed
4 oz. hard Cheddar cheese, grated

Roll out the pastry to a rectangle measuring about 12 × 15 inches. Sprinkle the grated cheese on top and fold the pastry into three, so that the cheese is layered between the pastry. Roll out again until the pastry measures about 10 × 12 inches and cut into thin strips, ¼ × 4 inches. Twist each of these and space out on damp baking sheets. Bake in a hot oven (425 deg. F. – Gas Mark 7) for 8–10 minutes until risen and golden. Remove from baking sheet, cool and serve. Makes about 100.

Raspberry Soufflé
1 8-oz. packet frozen raspberries, thawed
2 oz. icing sugar
½ oz. gelatine *dissolved in*
   ¼ pint water
3 eggs, separated
3 oz. castor sugar
¼ pint double cream, lightly whipped

Tie a greased, double thickness, sheet of greaseproof paper round a 6-inch soufflé dish. Sieve the raspberries, reserving a few for garnish and fold the icing sugar into the purée. Heat the gelatine in the water, over a pan of boiling water, and allow to cool slightly. Whisk the egg yolks and castor sugar together over hot water. Fold in the raspberry purée and gelatine, and cool. Fold in half the cream. Whisk the egg whites and fold into the mixture. Turn into prepared soufflé dish and leave to set. When set, remove the 'collar' carefully and decorate with the remaining whipped cream and raspberries. Serves 6.

Strawberry and Hazel Nut Torte
5 oz. plain flour
3 oz. butter or margarine
3½ oz. castor sugar
2 oz. hazel nuts, coarsely chopped
1 8-oz. packet frozen strawberries
½ pint double cream, lightly whipped

Sieve the flour, rub in the butter or margarine. Fold in half the sugar and the nuts, and knead the mixture together. Divide the mixture in half and press into two 7-inch circles on a well greased baking sheet. Bake in a moderately hot oven (375 deg. F. – Gas Mark 5) for 15–20 minutes or until golden brown. Allow to cool. Meanwhile sprinkle the strawberries with the remaining sugar and allow to thaw for about 1 hour. Reserve a few strawberries for decoration. Spread half the cream on one of the circles, place the fruit on the cream and cover with the second circle. Pipe the remaining cream on top and decorate with the remaining strawberries. Serves 5–6.

Florida Cheese Cake
For the crust:
2 oz. butter
1 oz. castor sugar
4 oz. digestive biscuits, crushed with a
    rolling pin
For the filling:
2 eggs, separated
2 oz. castor sugar
1 tablespoon undiluted frozen orange
    juice, thawed
8 oz. cottage cheese
½ pint double cream, lightly whipped
To decorate:
fresh orange segments
whipped cream

Melt butter in a pan, add sugar and crushed biscuits, mix well together. Line an 8-inch sandwich tin with foil. Press the biscuit mixture into the tin with a spoon, leave in refrigerator to set.
Beat egg yolks and sugar together, in a bowl over hot water, until thick and creamy. Add the undiluted orange juice. Allow to cool. Mash the cheese with a fork and add to mixture. Fold in the cream. Stiffly whisk egg whites and fold into mixture. Pour into the crumb base. Fold over the foil and freeze the cake until firm.
Decorate with fresh orange segments and whipped cream. Eat semi-frozen. Serves 6.

Cold Orange Soufflé
3 small eggs, separated
2 oz. castor sugar
half 6¼-oz. can undiluted frozen orange
    juice, thawed
2 tablespoons Cointreau
1 teaspoon lemon juice
½ oz. gelatine *dissolved in*
    2 tablespoons water
¼ pint double cream, lightly whipped
To decorate:
whipped cream
angelica
fresh orange segments or nuts

Tie a greased, double thickness, sheet of greaseproof paper round a 5-inch soufflé dish. Beat egg yolks with the sugar, in a bowl over a pan of boiling water, until thick and creamy. Remove from the heat and continue to whisk for a further few minutes. Whisk in the orange juice, Cointreau and lemon juice.
Melt gelatine in water in a small bowl over a pan of hot water, stir into the mixture. Fold in cream. Stiffly whisk egg whites and fold into mixture. Turn the orange mixture into the prepared soufflé dish and leave to set.
When set, remove the 'collar' carefully, and decorate with whipped cream, angelica, fresh orange segments or nuts if liked. Serves 4–5.

Florida Orange Jelly
1 6¼-oz. can frozen undiluted orange
    juice, thawed
2 cans water
½ oz. gelatine
1 apple, peeled, cored and roughly diced

Pour the orange juice into a bowl and add 1½ cans water. Dissolve the gelatine in the remaining ½ can of water in a basin over hot water. Allow to cool. When cooled, add gelatine to the orange juice with the diced apple. Pour into a mould and leave until set. Turn out and serve slightly chilled if possible. Serves 4.

Turn out each mousse carefully while still frozen
and lift with a palette knife onto a slice of swiss roll

Mousse party special decorated
with whipped cream and strawberries

Mousse Party Special
4 thick slices jam swiss roll
4 strawberry mousse tubs
¼ pint double cream, lightly whipped
8 oz. strawberries or raspberries

Place slices in the centres of four small glass plates. Turn out each mousse carefully while still frozen and lift with a palette knife on to a slice of swiss roll. Using a rose tube and large forcing bag, pipe cream rosettes round the base of each mousse. Decorate the edge with a few strawberries and place a single strawberry on top of each mousse.   Serves 4.

Variation

To make an interesting change, or when fresh berries are out of season, use a chocolate swiss roll and chocolate mousse tubs. Decorate in the same way with whipped cream, chocolate buttons or grated chocolate.

Tangy Apple Tart
1 7½-oz. packet frozen shortcrust pastry,
   thawed
For the filling:
1 oz. butter
2 oz. castor sugar
1 egg, beaten
1 teaspoon grated lemon rind
1 tablespoon lemon juice
2 large cooking apples, peeled and
   coarsely grated

Roll out the pastry and line a 7-inch flan ring.

Melt the butter, remove from the heat and add the remaining ingredients. Spoon the filling into the flan case. Cut the pastry trimmings into strips, ¼ inch wide, and make a lattice on the top of the flan. Bake in a moderately hot oven (400 deg. F. – Gas Mark 6) for about 40 minutes. Serve chilled with whipped cream.
                    Serves 4.

Lemon Meringue Tartlets
1 7½-oz. packet frozen shortcrust pastry,
   thawed
For the filling:
1½ oz. cornflour
½ pint water
grated rind and juice 1 large lemon
5 oz. castor sugar
2 eggs, separated

Roll out the pastry and cut into circles using a 3-inch cutter. Put into patty tins, prick well and bake 'blind' for 7–10 minutes in a moderate oven (350 deg. F. – Gas Mark 4). Blend the cornflour with the water, lemon rind and juice, 1 oz. sugar and egg yolks in a saucepan and bring to the boil, stirring. Cook for 3 minutes and spoon into the tarts. Whisk the egg whites until stiff, beat in half the remaining sugar and continue whisking until dry and firm. Fold in the rest of the sugar and pipe or spoon onto the tartlets. Bake in a slow oven (300 deg. F. – Gas Mark 2) for 20–30 minutes until meringue is firm. Remove from patty tins and cool.
                    Makes 18.

Grapefruit Zabaione

4 egg yolks
2 oz. castor sugar
3 tablespoons undiluted frozen grapefruit
    juice, thawed
2 tablespoons sweet sherry

Beat the egg yolks and sugar together in a bowl over a pan of boiling water until thick and creamy. Remove the bowl from the heat and gradually whisk in the grapefruit juice and sherry. Continue whisking until the mixture is thick again. Serve immediately in glasses or serve chilled with Langues de Chat. Serves 6.

Strawberry Eclairs

Allow 2 medium or 3 small strawberries for each éclair. Make a slit in the side of the frozen éclairs and allow to thaw. Cut the strawberries in half and place in the cream inside the éclairs. Serve.

Orange Honeys

2 oz. butter
2 oz. sugar
1 tablespoon frozen undiluted orange
    juice, thawed
1 tablespoon honey or golden syrup
4 oz. cornflakes

Place butter, sugar, orange juice and honey in a saucepan, bring to the boil and simmer for 2 minutes only. Gently stir in the cornflakes and mix thoroughly with the syrup. Spoon into paper bun cases and bake in a moderate oven (350 deg. F. – Gas Mark 4) for 5 minutes. Allow to cool thoroughly before storing in an airtight tin. Makes 24–36.

Peanut Tarts

1 7½-oz. packet frozen shortcrust pastry,
    thawed
For the filling:
raspberry or strawberry jam
1 egg white
4 oz. sugar
2 tablespoons desiccated coconut
3 oz. peanuts, coarsely chopped

Roll out pastry thinly and cut into circles using a 3-inch cutter. Put into patty tins. Place half a teaspoon of jam in the base of each. Combine the egg white, sugar, coconut and peanuts in a saucepan and mix thoroughly. Heat very gently until mixture is just lukewarm and place a heaped teaspoon of the topping in each case. Bake in a moderately hot oven (400 deg. F. – Gas Mark 6) for approximately 15 minutes. Makes 18.

Here are suggestions for planning menus to make the fullest use of the freezer

All the recipes marked with an asterisk are given in the preceding chapter. Use them when you need to plan appetising meals with the minimum of preparation time, using commercially frozen products which the freezer enables you to store in quantity.

BUFFET LUNCHEON

 Asparagus Rolls
*Salade Niçoise
*Prawn Salad
*Rice Salad
*Tourangelle
 Garlic Bread
 Chicken Joints
*Primavera Salad
 Tossed Green Salad
 Cassata
*Tangy Apple Tart and Cream
*Raspberry Soufflé

BUFFET SUPPER

*Cheese Twists
 Sausage Rolls
*Chicken Vol-au-Vents
*Crispy Cod Fries with Sweet and Sour Sauce
*Steaklet Kebabs
*Corn and Bacon Tarts
*Kipper Pizzas
 Sausages in Bacon
*Strawberry Eclairs
*Lemon Meringue Tartlets

FOUR DINNER PARTY MENUS

Iced Consommé
*Salmon with Cucumber Sauce
Asparagus
New Potatoes
Petits Pois
*Strawberry and Hazelnut Torte

*Trout Amandine
*Coq au Vin
Broccoli Spears
Potato Croquettes
*Florida Cheesecake

Potted Shrimps
*Beef Wellington
Whole Green Beans
Duchesse Potatoes
*Grapefruit Zabaione

Pâté
Breaded Scampi and Tartare Sauce
Chips
Broccoli Spears
*Orange Soufflé

CHILDREN'S HIGH TEA

*Cod Steak Crisps
*Souper Sausages
*Beefburger Bean Bake
*Cheesy Fish Fingers
Crispy Cod Fries
Sausage Savouries

*Florida Orange Jelly
*Peanut Tarts
*Orange Honeys
Mousse in Tubs
Dairy Cream Trifle
Eclairs

WEEK DAY MEALS

A busy working mother's plan for feeding her family from the freezer on week days, leaving her time for more elaborate cooking at the weekend.

Monday

Grilled Chicken Quarters
Grilled Mushrooms
Sweetcorn
New Potatoes

Fresh Fruit Salad and
Cream

Tuesday

Steak and Kidney Pie
Mixed Vegetables
Mashed Potato

Orange/Lemon Tub
Mousse with Mandarins

Wednesday

Braised Beef Slices
Horseradish Sauce
Roast Potatoes
Brussels Sprouts

Dairy Cream Trifle

Thursday

Chicken and Mushroom
Casserole
Potato Croquettes
Cauliflower

Pears and Hot Chocolate
Sauce

Friday

Fish and Chips
Tartare Sauce
Peas
Grilled Tomato Halves

Arctic Roll and Peaches

USEFUL THAWING TIME-TABLES

Cakes

Type of Cake
8-inch layer cake

1 layer, not iced	1–1¼ hours
2 layer, with ½-inch icing	2 hours
2 layer, with ¼-inch icing	1–1¼ hours
2 layer, with ⅛-inch icing	1–1¼ hours

Angel cake, sponge

whole cake	3–4 hours
wedges	1¼–1½ hours
Cupcakes	12–25 minutes

Dairy Foods

Dairy foods	Approx. refrigerator thawing time	Approx. room temperature thawing time
Eggs, whole	18–20 hours per ½ pt.	1½ hours
Eggs, yolks	18–20 hours per ½ pt.	1½ hours
Cream	8 hours per ¼ lb.	1½ hours
Cheese	8 hours per ¼ lb.	2–3 hours
Butter	2 hours per ½ lb.	30 minutes
Milk	18–20 hours per pt.	1½ hours

Vegetables

Vegetables	Approx. refrigerator thawing time	Approx. room temperature thawing time
Beetroot, young	9–10 hours per lb.	2–3 hours
Mushroom, caps	6–8 hours per lb.	2–3 hours
Peppers (sliced)	24 hours per lb.	1½ hours
Potatoes	8 hours per lb.	1½ hours

Meat

Meat	Approx. refrigerator thawing time	Approx. room temperature thawing time
Beef	5 hours per lb.	2 hours per lb.
Veal	5 hours per lb.	2 hours per lb.
Lamb	5 hours per lb.	2 hours per lb.
Pork	5 hours per lb.	Thaw in refrigerator only as de-frosting in a warm room can be dangerous.
Sausages	6 hours per lb.	1½–2 hours per lb.
Chops (½ inch thick)	6 hours per lb.	1–2 hours per lb.
Steaks (½ inch thick)	6 hours per lb.	1–2 hours per lb.
Steaks (1 inch thick)	8 hours per lb.	2–3 hours per lb.
Steaks (over 1 inch thick)	8–10 hours per lb.	3–4 hours per lb.
Poultry (whole)	See chart opposite for thawing poultry	
Chicken (portions)	5–6 hours per lb.	1 hour per lb.
Minced meat	10–12 hours per lb.	1–1½ hours per lb.
Meat patties	6 hours per lb.	1 hour per lb.

Offal

Sheep's heart	8–9 hours per lb.	1–1½ hours per lb.
Lamb's kidney	8–9 hours per lb.	1–1½ hours per lb.
Sliced liver	8–9 hours per lb.	½–¾ hour per lb.
Sliced sweetbreads	10 hours per lb.	¾–1 hour per lb.
Tripe	10–12 hours per lb.	1–1½ hours per lb.
Lamb's tongue	10–12 hours per lb.	1–1¼ hours per lb.

Game

Hare	5–6 hours per lb.	1½–2 hours per lb.
Rabbit	5–6 hours per lb.	1½–2 hours per lb.
Cooked meat stews and casseroles	8–10 hours per lb.	1–1½ hours per lb.

Fruit Purées

Fruit purées ½ pint packs	Refrigerator thawing time	Room temperature thawing time
Apple purée	6–8 hours	2–4 hours
Avocado purée	6–8 hours	2–4 hours
Banana purée	6–8 hours	2–4 hours

To thaw fruit juice allow 2–3 hours at room temperature or 4–6 hours in the refrigerator.

Fish

Fish	Approx. refrigerator thawing time	Approx. room temperature thawing time
Haddock	6–10 hours per lb.	3–5 hours per lb.
Halibut	6–10 hours per lb.	3–5 hours per lb.
Herring	6–10 hours per lb.	3–5 hours per lb.
Mackerel	6–10 hours per lb.	3–5 hours per lb.
Salmon	6–10 hours per lb.	3–5 hours per lb.
Turbot	6–10 hours per lb.	3–5 hours per lb.
Trout	6–10 hours per lb.	3–5 hours per lb.
Cod	6–10 hours per lb.	3–5 hours per lb.
Plaice	6–10 hours per lb.	3–5 hours per lb.
Sole	6–10 hours per lb.	3–5 hours per lb.
Whiting	6–10 hours per lb.	3–5 hours per lb.
Crab	10–12 hours per pint carton	3 hours per pint carton
Lobster	10–12 hours per pint carton	3 hours per pint carton
Oysters	8 hours	4–6 hours
Scallops	8 hours	4–6 hours
Shrimps	5–8 hours per 4 oz. pack	1½–2 hours per pint carton
Kippers	5 hours	2–2½ hours
Smoked Haddock	5 hours	2–2½ hours
Bloaters	5 hours	2–2½ hours

Bread and Sandwiches

Bread and sandwiches	Approx. refrigerator thawing time	Approx. room temperature thawing time
Uncooked bread dough	Overnight	5–6 hours
Baked bread	Overnight	
Baked rolls	Overnight	
Baked bread slices		2–3 minutes in toaster or under grill
Sandwiches		2½–3 hours
Canapés	1–2 hours	15–20 minutes

Poultry

Type	Thawing in the refrigerator
Chickens	
4 lb. and over	1–1½ days
Under 4 lb.	12–16 hours
Ducks	
3–5 lb.	1–1½ days
Geese	
4–14 lb.	1–2 days
Turkeys	
18 lb. and over	2–3 days
Under 18 lb.	1–2 days

Fruit

Fruit	Approx. refrigerator thawing time	Approx. room temperature thawing time
Soft fruits (skinless)		
Blackberries	6–7 hours	2–3 hours
Raspberries	6–7 hours	2–3 hours
Strawberries	6–7 hours	2–3 hours
Soft fruits (with tough skins)		
Avocado—whole	7–8 hours	3–4 hours
Apricots	7–8 hours	3–4 hours
Cherries	7–8 hours	3–4 hours
Cranberries	7–8 hours	3–4 hours
Currants	7–8 hours	3–4 hours
Damsons	7–8 hours	3–4 hours
Figs	7–8 hours	3–4 hours
Gooseberries	7–8 hours	3–4 hours
Grapes	7–8 hours	3–4 hours
Grapefruit segments	7–8 hours	3–4 hours
Peaches	7–8 hours	3–4 hours
Crisp fruits		
Apple slices	7–8 hours	3½–4 hours
Pear slices	7–8 hours	3½–4 hours
Rhubarb	7–8 hours	3½–4 hours

Index